LOYAL FORCES

LOYAL FORCES

The American Animals of World War II

TONI M. KISER AND LINDSEY F. BARNES

THE NATIONAL WORLD WAR II MUSEUM and

LOUISIANA STATE UNIVERSITY PRESS)((Baton Rouge

Published by Louisiana State University Press
Copyright © 2013 by Louisiana State University Press
All rights reserved
Manufactured in the United States of America
FIRST PRINTING

DESIGNER: Mandy McDonald Scallan
TYPEFACE: Whitman
PRINTER AND BINDER: Sheridan Books, Inc.

Frontispiece: Rex with Sgt. Amos Shaeffer in Italy.
Gift in memory of William F. Caddell, Sr. 2007.048.

Library of Congress Cataloging-in-Publication Data

Kiser, Toni M., 1981–
  Loyal forces : the American animals of World War II
/ Toni M. Kiser and Lindsey F. Barnes.
      p. cm.
  Includes bibliographical references.
  ISBN 978-0-8071-4996-6 (cloth : alk. paper) — ISBN
978-0-8071-4997-3 (pdf) — ISBN 978-0-8071-4998-0
(epub) — ISBN 978-0-8071-4999-7 (mobi) 1. Animals—War use—United States—History—20th century. 2. World War, 1939–1945. I. Barnes, Lindsey F.,
1980– II. Title.
  D810.A65K57 2013
  940.54'1—dc23

                          2012027796

The paper in this book meets the guidelines for per-
manence and durability of the Committee on Production Guidelines for Book Longevity of the Council on
Library Resources. ∞

For Ellie and Felix

CONTENTS

Preface ix

1. Dogs and War 1

2. The Army Mule 25

3. Pigeons 47

4. The Last Cavalry Charge 65

5. Loyal Forces on the Home Front 77

6. Foreign Encounters 93

7. Pets and Mascots 107

Selected Bibliography 123

PREFACE

As archivist and registrar at The National World War II Museum, we hold jobs that are closely associated with the museum's collection of photographs and artifacts. When we began our work at the museum in 2008, it was the photographs, stories, and equipment related to animals that piqued our interest. These were the items that caused us to turn to each other and say, "You have to see this!" The use of animals as both beasts of burden and companions struck us with wonder. Being lovers of all the world's creatures and coming from historical backgrounds, we were excited by the idea of better understanding the many ways that animals participated in and sacrificed for the wars of men, particularly World War II. In all our studies of that conflict, we had heard little about war dogs or messenger pigeons. The more we began to uncover about the topic, the more we wanted a way to tell their story.

In the summer of 2010 the museum opened the exhibit "Loyal Forces: The Animals of World War II," which we curated together. This book developed from that exhibit. Although we are not officially curators, we jumped at the chance to create an exhibit on what had become one of our favorite subjects. It was a great way to showcase the many artifacts and photographs we had discovered in the museum's collection. Although this book differs somewhat from the original exhibit by being limited to Americans' deployment of and experiences with animals, we hope that the general themes of loyalty, assistance, and comfort still shine through its images and stories. In the frightening and uncharted world of war, servicemen and women could count on the transport given by horses and mules, the protection offered by dogs, the communication delivered by pigeons, and the solace provided by mascots and pets. What follows are stories of the great deeds and contributions of American animals during World War II.

We would like to thank the many people who helped to make this book a reality. First and foremost, we are grateful to our editor, Margaret Lovecraft, who guided and directed us. Next, a huge thank-you to the World War II veterans who contributed their personal stories: Hiram Boone, Edwin Price Ramsey, and William Wynne. We would also like to thank Linda Good and Susan

Bahary, who offered their own photographs for reproduction. Several organizations gave us permission to use images from their archives, for which we are grateful: the U.S. Coast Guard Archive, the FBI, the American Historical Collection at the University of Manila, and the University of the Pacific Library.

This project relied heavily on the generosity of friends, coworkers, and family members, who took the time to read the text in its many stages. We especially appreciate the help of Eric Rivet, Michael Edwards, and Wanda Kiser.

Finally, we would like to thank Tom Czekanski for his support of both the "Loyal Forces" exhibit and this book.

LOYAL FORCES

U.S. Marine Corps dog handlers on patrol with Doberman pinschers on Iwo Jima, 1945. *Gift of Barbara Meek, 2002.141.*

1. Dogs and War

Dogs were used in times of war even before the invention of gunpowder. Romans used them to charge into battle and attack the enemy. Native Americans used them as both pack and draft animals as well as sentry animals. In the Middle Ages, dogs were sent into battle equipped with their own armor. Modern European societies have long-established traditions of using dogs in war. In World War I, the French, the Belgians, and the Germans used dogs as messengers, medics, and pack animals. The United States, however, never had a war-dog program until the onset of World War II. And the only working dogs in the U.S. military at the start of that war were sled dogs used in Alaska when the snowy and icy terrain was impassable by vehicle. It was through the forward thinking of some in the U.S. military with the enthusiastic support of dog fanciers that the U.S. government initiated a war-dog training program. Supporters of the program envisioned the various ways that dogs could be useful in both combat and non-combat roles.

Advocates of war dogs were quick to point out the many characteristics that made dogs useful in war. First of these is a dog's respect for humans. Good dogs are always eager to please their mas-

ters. As a result, they can become highly trained according to their intelligence level. Dogs are also docile and watchful by nature. Although a dog's eyesight is not particularly good, its ability to perceive movement is exceptional. Dogs have acute senses of hearing and smell and can act with great speed, making them valuable companions in times of war. These characteristics of watchfulness and docility, combined with highly developed senses, give them an extraordinary ability to notice, find, and observe many things a human cannot.

In January 1942, Dogs for Defense, Inc. (DFD) was established as a national organization to help procure dogs for war-training purposes. Although some dogs were purchased, it was largely through the patriotic donations of dog owners that dogs were acquired. The DFD not only obtained but also trained the dogs. The U.S. Army's quartermaster general then received the trained animals from the DFD and turned them over to the Plant Protection Branch and Inspection Division.

The primary use of dogs was originally envisioned as sentries at civilian war plants and quartermaster depots. As it turned out, the DFD program, which was run on a voluntary basis, was

Alene Erlanger meets with Maj. Gen. E. B. Gregory to discuss sentry dogs for industrial plant security. *National Archives photo.*

Clyde Porter gives his dog Junior to Dogs for Defense. Most of the United States' 20,000 war dogs were volunteered for service by their owners. *National Archives photo.*

unable to keep up with the demand for sentry dogs. Furthermore, there was no central training facility or method, so standardized training of the dogs was impossible. Therefore, in late 1942, a new program was adopted. DFD was still responsible for the procurement of dogs, but sentry-dog training would now take place through the Remount Branch of the Quartermaster Corps, rather than the Plant Protection Branch. Other types of dog training were also initiated, including training for roving patrol dogs, messenger dogs, and sled dogs. And it was determined that in the fall of 1942 the Remount Branch would train dogs not only for the U.S Army, but also for the U.S. Navy and the U.S. Coast Guard.

To handle the demand for trained sentry dogs, the quartermaster general set up war-dog reception and training centers. These centers were to receive the animals from DFD, give them a thorough physical examination, classify them for the type of work for which they were suited, and provide the training necessary to make them usable to the army. These centers were also responsible for training the dog handlers and making sure that there were always adequate numbers of trained handlers.

Training centers were established at Front Royal, Virginia; Fort Robinson, Nebraska; Camp Rimini, Montana; and San Carlos, California. In April 1943 another center was opened on Cat Island, off the coast of Gulfport, Mississippi. The Front Royal and Fort Robinson locations were part of permanent installations. Others were located strategically based on the type of training needed. For instance, Camp Rimini was used solely for training sled dogs, and Cat Island was used to simulate the jungle environment of the Pacific theater.

While the army's Quartermaster Corps was training dogs for the army, the navy, and the coast guard, the U.S. Marine Corps set off on its

Dogs are inducted into the army at Front Royal, Virginia. *National Archives photo.*

own path to train war dogs. For a short time, the marines recruited dogs from private citizens, but as the war progressed, they also turned to DFD and the army's Quartermaster Corps to procure dogs for training. The marine corps set up its own training center at Camp Lejeune, North Carolina. At first the marines also worked in conjunction with the Doberman Pinscher Club of America to acquire Dobermans for military service. Because the marine corps had an initial preference for male Doberman pinschers, these dogs became associated with the marines and were nicknamed "Devil Dogs" for their fighting tenacity. Since the U.S. Marine Corps focuses on combat operations,

they concentrated their training on scout and messenger dogs, which they thought would be more likely to reduce marine casualties.

Another notable difference between army and marine corps training was the dog handlers themselves. The army used soldiers from the Quartermaster Corps as dog handlers. These soldiers did not receive the extra and more intense training that combat soldiers received. The marine corps, on the other hand, recognized that the best use of the dogs was as an extension of a well-trained marine. The marine dog handlers spent half of their training time with dogs and the other half in intensive marine-corps scout-sniper training.

A WAR DOG JOURNEY

In a typical situation, a patriotic owner would volunteer a dog for war service by contacting Dogs for Defense, which had many regional offices where dogs could be taken. DFD obtained 18,000 dogs during the three years it was in charge of procurement for the Quartermaster Corps. Donated dogs were given a battery of medical tests to ensure they were fit for training and military duties. Dogs that did not pass the medical tests were returned to their owners; those that were selected were sent on to one of the army or marine corps training centers. There they would be subjected to more medical exams and intelligence testing. Dogs that passed were assigned to a regiment and a handler to begin their military training.

Several qualities make a good war dog. First, a dog must have keen use of all its senses. Smell and hearing are key, but sight is also important. Second, a dog must not be too sensitive or "shy." Rather, it must possess the right balance of fear and aggression so that it can be trained in the presence of artillery and gun fire. A war dog must also be intelligent. A dog's intelligence is evaluated by the quickness with which it learns and retains training. But a dog must also exhibit a willingness to respond to a trainer's commands, and the trainer must provide the right motivation for a dog to live up to its potential. Although the army and marine corps had breeds of dogs that each preferred, neither discriminated on the basis of gender. Dogs of both sexes performed equally well in training and combat situations.

ACCEPTABLE BREEDS

The army's requirements for dogs were at first limited to purebred animals, of either sex, between the ages of one and five, physically sound,

Tech. Sgt. Floyd Harmon stands with a newly received war dog. Harmon was stationed at Fort Robinson, Nebraska, where he received dogs donated to Dogs for Defense. *Courtesy Linda (Lindy) Harmon Good, in memory of Floyd Eugene Harmon, K-9 Corps, Fort Robinson, Nebraska.*

and with the characteristics of a watchdog. Later these requirements would be relaxed to include cross breeds whose ancestry could be traced and that still exhibited a particular breed's characteristics. In all, thirty-two breeds and their crosses were considered acceptable, including:

Airedale
Alaskan malamute
Belgian sheepdog
Boxer
Bullmastiff
Collie
Dalmatian
Doberman pinscher

English springer spaniel
German shepherd
Giant schnauzer
Great Dane
Irish water spaniel
Labrador retriever
Rottweiler
Saint Bernard
Siberian husky
Standard poodle

By 1944 the list would shrink to five breeds that had proven to work best in military roles: German and Belgian shepherds, Dobermans, collies, and giant schnauzers. In addition, the malamute, Inuit sled dog, and Siberian husky were still preferred as sled dogs.

As the war-dog program developed, the true test of all the breeds would come in actual combat. First Lt. William T. Taylor, commander of the U.S. Marine Corps 2nd War Dog Platoon, which saw intense combat on Guam, dutifully reported on his experiences with various breeds. Despite the push by fanciers of the Doberman pinscher, the dog did not stand up well in combat. On the other hand, Taylor felt that the German shepherd performed exceptionally during combat and seemed to have a stronger constitution, making it more stable and with more stamina than other breeds.

TATTOOS

Much as men and women in the service were given serial numbers, dogs also received a number that followed them throughout their military career. A dog's number was tattooed in its ear or on its flank. The army utilized the Preston tattooing system, which allowed them to mark four thousand animals with an assigned letter. A000 would be the first, then A001, and so on, until A999. Then the letter placing would change to 0A00, then 0A01 through 9A99, and so on. This system was highly efficient and gave the Quartermaster Corps an ordered approach to keeping track of a dog and all its records. A considerable amount of time and effort was spent to make sure that dogs were as well accounted for as servicemen. They were given ranks, and their time in the service was tracked just like that of a soldier or marine.

TRAINING

All war-dog training began with basic obedience. Dogs had to know the elementary commands sit, stay, and heel. At first these commands would be given verbally by the handler, but it was crucial that the dogs also learn to obey commands given with hand signals. Any sound could alert the enemy to the presence of a patrol, so nonverbal communication between the dog and its handler was critical to their success. To this end, dogs were trained not to bark or growl. They were also trained on obstacle courses, where they were required to jump, climb, crawl, wade, and swim to reach their objective.

After a dog had mastered basic obedience, it had to become accustomed to the various military procedures it would encounter. These ran the gamut from riding in jeeps and trucks to wearing a gas mask or a muzzle. One of the most important parts of the dog's training was desensitizing the animal to gun and artillery fire. Initially dogs did not receive this training, and they suffered in actual combat conditions. A dog was considered desensitized to noise when a small-caliber pistol could be shot over its head without the dog flinching. To accomplish this, weapons would be fired at a distance from the dog and slowly brought closer, with the caliber gradually increasing as well. *War Dogs* (U.S. War Depart-

Military policemen and dogs pose on part of the training course all dogs had to complete to become war dogs. *Courtesy Linda (Lindy) Harmon Good, in memory of Floyd Eugene Harmon, K-9 Corps, Fort Robinson, Nebraska.*

Most invasions took place on the islands of the Pacific, so it was essential that all dogs be able to swim. This dog completes part of the training course at Fort Robinson, Nebraska. *Courtesy Linda (Lindy) Harmon Good, in memory of Floyd Eugene Harmon, K-9 Corps.*

Sentry dogs were taught to attack when given the proper command. Here a handler trains his dog to attack the enemy. *Courtesy Linda (Lindy) Harmon Good, in memory of Floyd Eugene Harmon, K-9 Corps, Fort Robinson, Nebraska.*

ment Technical Manual 10-396) states, "It is best to start this training when the dog is engaged in some activity which absorbs his attention, such as eating, or during training periods. Thus the dog subconsciously becomes accustomed to distant gunfire and firing can be resumed closer and closer without unduly disturbing him."

Once a dog completed basic obedience training, military procedure training, and noise desensitization, it would begin specialized training for its specific job. Dogs were screened to determine which job they were best suited to perform. Scout, sentry, and patrol dogs learned when to alert their handler to the presence of another person. Additionally, scout dogs learned how to work off leash. Central to training was the collar. The dog wore a certain type of collar while training or working and another type of collar while resting. Dogs soon learned the type of behavior expected of them when a specific collar was worn.

DUTIES

The U.S. Army and U.S. Marine Corps trained dogs for various types of work, primarily sled and pack, sentry and roving patrol, messenger, scout, and mine detection work.

SLED AND PACK DOGS

At the start of World War II, the only working dogs in the U.S. military were sled and pack dogs working primarily in the snowy and icy terrains of the northern United States including Alaska. They were trained to pull sleds with both passengers and supplies. In the fall of 1942, when the Army Remount Branch took over dog-training efforts, a special training center was established at Camp Rimini in Montana exclusively for pack and sled dogs. Only special breeds of dogs were considered for this type of work because of the

PFC Rez P. Hester of the U.S. Marine Corps' 7th War Dog Platoon on Iwo Jima takes a nap while Butch stands guard. Trained and sent into battle together, war dogs and their partners developed mutual loyalty, protectiveness, and love. *National Archives photo.*

often harsh conditions they would have to endure. Sled dogs had to be able to withstand temperatures as low as -60° F., and pack dogs had to be able to pull loads of up to five hundred pounds. In some cases, pack and sled dogs were of greater use than mules and horses because of their ability to pull over icy terrain. Dogs trained at Camp Rimini were sent to Newfoundland in 1942 and to Greenland in 1943. They worked mostly to search for and rescue downed air crews. In all, these teams would rescue almost one hundred downed men and move thousands of pounds of equipment.

SENTRY AND ROVING PATROL DOGS

The attack on Pearl Harbor in December 1941 and the need to protect the vast American coastline as well as war plants, manufacturing facilities, and military installations led to the use of dogs for sentry duty. Advocates pointed out that the use of dogs attached to coast-guard beach patrols could prevent landings like those of German agents on the Atlantic and Gulf coasts in 1942. Dogs enhanced the efficiency of sentry work by supplementing a human's limited powers of hearing with their superior sense of smell and hearing.

Sentry dogs were used mainly for interior guard duty and beach patrols. They were trained to work on a leash and either posted at a specific spot with a handler or sent out to canvass a certain area. Though their training was less intense than that of other working dogs, they needed to be moderately intelligent, willing, and somewhat aggressive. Sentry dogs were trained to accompany both military and civilian patrols in various conditions and to give warning through barking or growling at the approach of another person. Sentry dogs were restrained from actually attacking unless the intruder threatened the handler.

A special type of sentry dog was the attack dog. Attack dogs were taught not merely to warn of another person's presence, but also to work off leash and attack on command. The program to train attack dogs was held at Cat Island, eight miles south of Gulfport, Mississippi. It was an ideal location for the training of dogs in a jungle-like environment. The head of the program was a Swiss national who maintained that packs of dogs could be trained to flush out Japanese soldiers that could not be taken by normal means. However, the trainer's tactics quickly came into question, and his inability to produce effective results swiftly ended the program. All dogs were given sentry training, and even scout dogs in combat zones performed sentry duties.

MESSENGER DOGS

Stories of dogs serving as messengers date as far back as the Civil War. During World War I, every country involved in the conflict except the United States utilized dogs, especially as messen-

Chips. *Gift of Regan Forrester, 2002.337.*

One of the most famous war dogs was Chips, a German shepherd/husky/collie mix. He was donated by Edward J. Wren of Pleasantville, New York, and trained at Front Royal, Virginia, in 1942. Chips was among the first dogs to be shipped overseas. He was assigned to the 3rd Infantry Division and served with that unit in North Africa, Sicily, Italy, France, and Germany along with his handler, Pvt. John R. Powell. Although trained as a sentry dog, Chips was known on one occasion by members of the 30th Infantry Regiment to break away from his handler and attack a pillbox containing an enemy machine-gun crew in Sicily. He attacked one Italian soldier, biting and slashing his arms and throat. The rest of the Italian crew was so frightened that they surrendered. Chips was also credited with being directly responsible for the capture of numerous enemy soldiers by alerting to their presence. In recognition of his service, Chips was awarded the Silver Star and the Purple Heart, although both were later revoked because of a military policy that did not allow commendations to be awarded to animals. Chips returned to Front Royal in October 1945, where he went through a demilitarizing process before being returned to his original owners.

On Iwo Jima, U.S. Marine Cpl. Virgil Burgess instructs his messenger dog, Prince. Notice the special messenger pouch Prince wears to deliver messages. *National Archives photo.*

gers. When properly trained, these dogs could indirectly save many lives. They carried messages four to five times faster than the average soldier on foot. Dogs have a much lower profile than humans, making them harder to see and more difficult to shoot. The equipment the dog needed was minimal—only a small canister around the neck. The dogs and their handlers could be trained in fourteen weeks. As the United States prepared to train messenger dogs in 1943, they sought help from the British, who had had great success with these dogs during World War I. Messenger dogs were the only dogs assigned two handlers. They were trained to go from one handler to the other to deliver and retrieve messages. They often traveled through dense jungles, sometimes under fire, and over considerable distances.

On New Guinea in December of 1943, com-manders gave messenger dogs a significant test. They raced a marine and a dog in heavy jungle to see which would deliver a message first. It took the trained messenger dog just four and a half minutes to cut through the jungle while the marine did not emerge for another eleven minutes.

SCOUT DOGS

The scout dog was one of the most prominent and important of the war dogs. These dogs were highly intelligent and intensely trained. The bond with their handlers was extremely strong, and upon the death of a handler it was not uncommon for a dog to defend his body. Used primarily in the Pacific, these dogs would walk up to twenty-five yards in front of a column of marines or soldiers. When the dog sensed an enemy sol-

Buster, a U.S. Army messenger dog with F Company, 155th Infantry Regiment, 39th Infantry Division, was a collie credited with saving seventeen lives. Messenger dogs were essential to many missions in the thick jungles of the Pacific, where radio signals could not penetrate the dense foliage. Buster was on patrol with F Company on the Indonesian island of Morotai when the patrol was surrounded by Japanese soldiers and pinned down by gunfire. Buster managed to avoid the heavy machine-gun and mortar fire as he ran back to headquarters, where he delivered the message about the endangered soldiers. He was then given a message to take back to the surrounded men: "Hold your position!" He returned to the company under fire. Reinforcements soon arrived and were able to rout the enemy.

Sandy fought in the Gloucester campaign and was handled by Sgts. Guy C. Sheldon and Menzo J. Brown. One of Sandy's most outstanding missions took place near Turzi Point as troops were advancing toward an airstrip. The units were held up by Japanese pillboxes. Communication via radio and walkie-talkies was down, so the troops could not call for artillery to help them fight the Japanese. Sergeant Brown sent Sandy with a message back to the battalion command post. Sandy had not seen Sergeant Sheldon since the night before, and the headquarters had moved to a new location since the dog left. Despite these obstacles, Sandy found his way to the command post and to Sheldon's foxhole. Sandy traveled through tall jungle grass, swam across a river, and ran through mortar and artillery fire to find Sheldon. Because of Sandy's successful delivery of the message, artillery fire was directed at the Japanese pillboxes and U.S. troops were permitted to move forward.

dier, it would give a signal or "alert" to its handler. The column would then engage the enemy before being seen.

The selection process for silent scout dogs was rigorous. Criteria included high intelligence, willingness, aggressiveness, and energy, as well as some sensitivity. The crucial feature of a scout dog is the "alert" the dog gives the handler to make the presence of another person known. This can be a tenseness to its body, raised hackles, ears pricked up, or some other sign an observant handler would recognize. Keeping dogs and handlers together from training through combat allowed each handler to gain this intimate knowledge of his dog and its signs.

Scout dogs were the most requested dogs in the war-dog program. Their ability to alert to the enemy saved countless lives. Both fighting men and their commanders quickly learned to respect the dogs, their handlers, and the work they accomplished.

MINE DETECTION DOGS

As American forces fought in North Africa, the German army periodically stalled their advance by using nonmetallic landmines. Electronic mine detectors, which easily identified metallic landmines, were useless against these new types of mines. Aware of some British success using dogs to detect landmines, the U.S. Army began an "M-dog" training program. These dogs were trained at the Cat Island facility, primarily through a method of repulsion or aversion. To teach the

A marine handler directs his scout dog to the entrance of a cave on Iwo Jima in 1945. If an enemy lurks inside, the dog will signal its handler. *National Archives photo.*

dogs how to detect buried mines and trip wires, trainers exploited the dogs' inherent sense of safety. When a dog came upon a training mine or trip wire, it would receive an electric shock. This would teach the dog to be wary of anything buried in the ground. If a dog came upon something, it learned to stop, thus alerting the handler to the presence of a mine.

In initial testing phases, the dogs missed 20 percent of mines that were buried and alerted 20 percent of the time when there was no mine. At first, these seemed like acceptable amounts.

Unfortunately, when it came time for M-dogs to perform in the field, the casualties of handlers and dogs were high. Their overall success rate was slim, and their deployments to North Africa in 1943 and Italy in 1944 were a failure. At that time, trainers and military leaders did not know that they could train the dogs to smell the explosives in a mine.

M-dogs were taught to look for disturbances on the ground or to detect human scent in turned earth. Their training had not accounted for the dead bodies that would be present in combat

Andy, a two-year-old Doberman pinscher donated to the marine corps by Theodore A. Wiedmann, was commended for outstanding performance of duty in action against the enemy on Bougainville Island, Solomon Islands. Andy made the landing with the marines on Empress Augusta Bay on November 1, 1943. *Gift of Charles Ives, 2011.102.*

Andy, a Doberman pinscher, deployed with M Company of the 3rd Marine Raider Battalion. He was trained by Pvts. Robert E. Lansley and John B. Mahoney to work off leash. Andy was considered an easy dog to read because his hackles bristled when he alerted to enemy forces. There were no marine casualties on Andy's patrols. Lansley and Mahoney had complete faith in Andy's ability to spot whatever was out there.

On one particular patrol, Andy moved with his two handlers beyond the lines into heavy foliage. Andy was about twenty-five yards out front when he stopped short and looked to the left and right. The two marines crept up along a little trail behind Andy and spotted two machine-gun nests, one on each side of the trail. The handlers started shooting, and Lansley threw two grenades. When it was all over, eight Japanese soldiers were dead. The destruction of the machine-gun nests by Andy and his handlers permitted that entire sector of the line to move forward.

zones or for the noises of gun, mortar, and artillery fire. These major distractions severely impaired the dogs' ability to work. Furthermore, the aversion or repulsion training technique was a nonviable method; dogs usually respond better to positive-reinforcement training techniques. The dogs and their handlers were by no means responsible for the failure of the M-dog program. Rather, lack of understanding of the dogs' capability, ineffective training techniques, and the military's push for immediate success brought about the demise of the program. The accomplishments of sentry, scout, and messenger dogs were staggering, but mine detection dogs—through no fault of their own—were the disappointment of the new war-dog training program.

COMBAT

The army's Quartermaster Corps (QMC) trained over 10,000 dogs, most of which were used on the home front for sentry duty. However, more than 1,800 dogs trained by the QMC were sent into combat starting in 1942. Likewise, the U.S. Marine Corps sent into combat over 1,000 dogs trained at their Camp Lejeune facility. Unfortunately, many commanders were unfamiliar with war dogs and how to use them to their advantage. Seven QMC war-dog platoons were sent to the European theater of operations, but they would not have much success. In 1943 the QMC sent a detachment of six scout dogs and two messenger dogs to operate in the Pacific theater as a test of their value in combat conditions.

Private John C. Tanner, of Huntsville, Alabama, and war dog Blitz-Kong search for Japanese soldiers and sailors in caves on Iwo Jima. This cave, running a quarter into the cliff and having several built-in rooms, was thought to be a Japanese naval command post. *National Archives photo.*

Japanese troops were deeply entrenched on many islands in the Pacific theater. Thousands of Japanese soldiers were hiding in caves and in the dense jungles. These troops would lie in wait for patrolling marines and soldiers and ambush them before the troops detected their presence. One of the first tests of war-dog platoons took place on the Pacific island of New Britain. Here, marine war dogs attached to the Sixth Army first worked on sentry duty. Once a beachhead was established, the dogs and their handlers began conducting patrols. They went on forty-eight patrols in fifty-three days while on the island, with two hundred Japanese soldiers captured or killed through these patrols. This early success set the standard for what could be expected—and what could not—from a K-9 detachment.

The use of dogs increased dramatically at the beginning of 1944. The Pacific island-hopping campaign brought U.S. forces to the island of Bougainville in November 1943, where the initial assault included the 1st Marine War Dog Platoon. This platoon patrolled the island for three months, and although two dogs were lost, no handlers were killed while on a patrol. This mission was vital to the continued success of the war-dog training program. Both Maj. Gen. Roy S. Geiger, commander of the U.S. ground forces on Bougainville, and Maj. Gen. Allen H. Turnage, marine division commander, called the use of the 1st War Dog Platoon an "unqualified success." Both army and marine war dogs participated in landings all across the Pacific in the island-hopping campaign. The adjacent map portrays just a portion of the islands where dogs were used.

PROBLEMS TO OVERCOME

There were many hurdles for the army, the handlers, and the dogs to overcome as the war-dog program first got underway. One of the largest obstacles for dogs and their handlers was that infantry commanders often lacked an understanding of how best to use war dogs. This meant that war-dog platoons could not always meet their full potential. A vital element to the success of these specialized platoons was communication between war-dog platoon commanders and the commanders of ground troops. Ground commanders needed to know what a dog could and could not be expected to do. Dogs and handlers were often sent into areas where their skills could not be used effectively. For instance, in February 1945 scout dogs attached to the 87th Infantry Regiment, 10th Mountain Division, in Italy were sent on a patrol. Because the ground commander did not give adequate notice to the dog handlers, the handlers were unable to brief patrol leaders

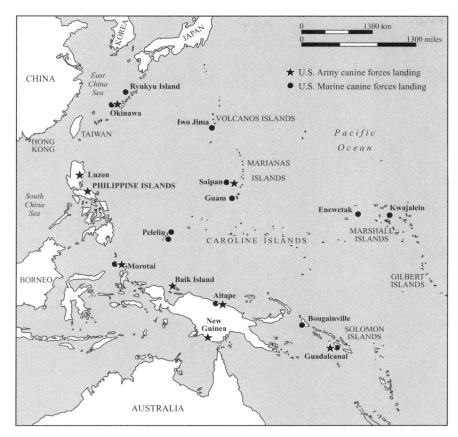

Pacific and Far East map noting some of the island landings of U.S. Army and Marine Corps war-dog platoons. *Map by Mary Lee Eggart.*

This marine corps war dog was killed by an artillery blast on the Iwo Jima beachhead. *National Archives photo.*

about what to expect. Winds that day were moving scents away from the dogs, so that they could not detect the presence of enemy forces. When this information was given to the commanding officer, it was disregarded. Not far into the patrol, the soldiers were pinned down by machine-gun fire for nearly two hours.

Lack of understanding and of communication were only two of the problems the war-dog program needed to overcome. The army and marine corps sent war-dog platoons to Guadalcanal, New Guinea, the Philippines, Okinawa, Guam, Iwo Jima, and many other combat zones. Often, war dogs and their handlers were met with ridicule

Kurt was a Doberman pinscher whose bravery saved the lives of 250 marines on the island of Guam. He alerted to Japanese soldiers lying in wait on a jungle hillside above the Asan Point beachhead. His handler, PFC Allen Jacobson, killed two Japanese soldiers before a mortar shell exploded near them. Those Japanese soldiers were part of a much larger force. Kurt's discovery of the outpost kept the 21st Marine Regiment from stumbling directly into the main body of enemy soldiers. Unfortunately, the mortar shell tore a large chunk out of Kurt's back. With his spine exposed and surgery impossible, he suffered for most of the day before succumbing to his wounds. His sacrifice led to his likeness being cast in bronze to memorialize all the dogs who gave their lives for the liberation of Guam.

Always Faithful, created by artist Susan Bahary, is a memorial to the marine war dogs of World War II and to all war dogs and handlers. It is the only official U.S. memorial at the war-dog cemetery in Guam and features a bronze statue on a granite base inscribed with the names of the twenty-five dogs that died in the fighting on Guam. The figure at the top of *Always Faithful* is modeled after Kurt. *Courtesy Susan Bahary.*

★

Snyder with his truck, Africa, 1944. *Gift of Howard M. Snyder, 2012.259.*

Technical Sgt. Howard R. Snyder was a truck driver for the Headquarters and Service Company of the 817th Engineer Aviation Battalion. He participated in many battles with the unit from Tunisia to the Rhineland. While on the island of Corsica, he found a small dog in an anti-aircraft gun emplacement, and rescued her from the combat taking place around the emplacement. He dubbed her the "Duchess of Corsica," or "Duchess" for short. The two became quick and steadfast companions. Duchess always rode next to Snyder in the truck, slept with him in his tent, and took cover with him under the truck when there was shelling or gunfire.

Duchess would be with Snyder for the remainder of the war, and would return to the United States with him aboard a liberty ship. Upon their return, Snyder made Duchess her own "uniform" using an army blanket and some of his insignia. She proudly marched in her uniform with Snyder at the first Memorial Day parade held in Westbury, Long Island, after the war. Snyder's son Howard M. Snyder remembers that his father was devoted to Duchess for her whole life. She lived to be eighteen years old.

One of the most famous war dogs was the messenger dog Caesar, a German shepherd who served during the Bougainville campaign. Caesar was with M Company of the 3rd Marine Raider Battalion, whose job was to hold a road block on the Piva Trail. Because of dense foliage, radios were unable to send or receive signals. Caesar provided a vital communications link, completing eleven messenger missions.

Caesar was not only an accomplished messenger dog, but also a valuable sentry dog. Three days into the Bougainville campaign, Caesar rushed out of the foxhole he shared with one of his handlers, PFC John Mayo. Mayo called the dog back, and as he was returning, a Japanese sniper shot Caesar. A firefight ensued, but Caesar had disappeared. He was later found with his other handler, PFC John Kleeman. The bullet hit too close to his heart to operate, but despite his wound Caesar survived and returned to duty three weeks later.

PFC John Kleeman and messenger dog Caesar on the west coast of Bougainville. Notice the bullet wound below Caesar's left shoulder, received during a Japanese attack. *National Archives photo.*

and resentment from infantry troops when they arrived in combat areas. Ground troops did not see the benefits of having scout dogs on patrols or sentry dogs on post at night. The initial lack of combat training for army dog handlers created further resentment among the ranks. However, the army would soon use the marine corps model and train handlers from the outset as infantrymen in addition to their dog-handling training. This afforded the handlers some trust and respect from the fighting men they worked alongside. As the war progressed and the dogs began to demonstrate their abilities to alert to the enemy, these perceptions would change. It took several patrols

for infantrymen and commanders to come to respect and understand how scout and messenger dogs could be used to their benefit, but by the end of the war, many men's lives had been saved by a scout dog's alert or a messenger dog's maneuverability.

There were some things only experience could teach, and the army itself had to adapt its training methods to lessons learned in the field. At first, dog trainers did not account for changes in wind direction and velocity, heat and humidity, and the concentration of human scents as factors affecting a dog's ability to alert to enemy soldiers. There was also a common perception

A marine and his dog sleep wherever and whenever possible—here, in a foxhole on Okinawa. *Time Life Pictures/Getty Images.*

that the dogs were indefatigable, but in reality, dogs needed rest just like the soldiers. Dogs that are tired lose interest in working, and their senses become compromised. It was important for handlers and commanders to make sure dogs were given rest time. Handlers gradually learned when their dogs were and were not able to work effectively, and communicated this to their commanders.

SUCCESS

QMC and U.S. Marine Corps war-dog platoons would find success in other island campaigns besides New Britain. On Morotai and other islands, where dense jungle conditions made radios inoperable, messenger dogs could maintain communications. And patrol dogs soon proved

their value. In September 1944 on Morotai, 31st Infantry Division soldiers came under sniper fire from the Japanese, who were deeply entrenched in the thick jungle. The 26th QMC War Dog Platoon provided the tactical edge to combat the Japanese. None of the 250 patrols accompanied by the war-dog platoon were ambushed by the Japanese. During the liberation of Guam, the 2nd and 3rd U.S. Marine War Dog Platoons went on more than 450 patrols. Dogs alerted on 130 of those patrols, resulting in 203 enemy soldiers killed. Unfortunately, twenty-five dogs were killed during the initial invasion and the mop-up operations.

By the time American troops reached the Philippines in January 1945, dogs were in great demand. Everyone wanted to go on patrol with a war dog and to have one in the foxhole next to him. The first dogs entered the Philippine campaign in January. From January to April 1945, dogs from the 25th and 26th QMC War Dog Platoons worked continuously on the island of Luzon. Initially these dogs were attached to the 169th Infantry Regiment; however, after two weeks of mediocre performance owing to patrol leaders not understanding the capabilities of scout and messenger dogs, the 26th War Dog Platoon was transferred to the 27th Infantry Division. Commanders of the 27th were much more familiar with dogs and used the platoon to great success. The commanding officer of the 26th War Dog Platoon noted that the dogs were considerably well used and that there were more requests for dogs than could be filled. In a report to the Sixth Army commander he stated, "Had more dogs been available, the number of lives saved would have been proportionately larger." As word of the success of the war-dog platoons spread and commanders became better informed about their use, divisions began requesting scout and messenger dogs as permanent assignments.

MEDICAL SUPPLIES AND THE WAR-DOG HOSPITAL

As the war-dog training program was so new, very little equipment and supplies specific to the dogs' needs had been developed. Medical supplies were no exception. The bandages, sutures, and medicines used to equip combat medics were those used to stock veterinary offices and treat wounded or sick dogs back home. Jungle conditions were harsh, and both the dogs and the handlers suffered from the intense heat and biting insects. Platoon veterinarians had to develop new methods to treat injuries and diseases, including using local dogs as blood donors for wounded war dogs.

Hookworm was one of the most common parasites to plague the war-dog platoons. Hook-worms bore holes in the sides of a dog's intestines and feed off the blood. This loss of blood causes severe anemia and eventually kills the dog. Using stomach tubes and butyl chloride every two weeks, veterinarians were able to keep many of the dogs healthy. However, there were times when dogs could not get worming treatments in time, and other methods were used to treat the parasitic infestation. One method was to transfuse blood from healthy dogs to those suffering from anemia. Only so much blood can be taken from one dog, so veterinarians turned to the local dog population, which they called "boonie dogs." Many of these dogs had developed an immunity to the hookworms and did not suffer ill effects from the infestation.

Heartworms were also present in the jungle, and veterinarians used simple blood tests to detect them. Treatment for heartworm infestation was complicated, since deworming a dog too quickly can cause toxemia and kill the dog. Heartworm treatments had to be done slowly and under close supervision. Lt. William Putney, commander of the 2nd and 3rd U.S. Marine War Dog Platoons, treated 440 war dogs from his platoons for heartworms in 1945 and 1946.

Proper food and clean water were essential to the care of war dogs. However, many supply officers had no idea how to stock a war-dog platoon for combat conditions. Lieutenant Putney received only enough dog food for a month as he was getting ready to ship out to the Pacific theater. Once on the front lines, dog rations were supplemented with horse and mule meat as well as fresh vegetables and cereals. However, those items were not always available in combat conditions. Soldiers on the front lines relied on C-rations with individual canned and precooked food for sustenance when fresh food was not available. Dogs therefore also relied on them. Fresh water was also key to a dog's health. Great strides

Lt. William Putney treats a wounded dog. *National Archives photo.*

mon diseases and basic care needs. Veterinarians had to not only keep their dogs healthy, but also act as combat medics for animals wounded in combat. Emergency surgeries to remove bullets and shrapnel were commonplace. Once the Japanese learned that the dogs were giving away their positions, snipers began to target the scout dogs. The marine corps war-dog platoons lost twenty-seven dogs to combat injuries and disease, while five were listed as missing in action. Dog handlers also suffered; 16 of the 110 men in the 2nd and 3rd U.S. Marine Corps war-dog platoons were killed in action, and more than 40 were wounded. By November 1943, only 25 of the original 110 handlers were still in action; all the others had been killed, wounded, or evacuated.

RETURNING HOME

In all, over 10,000 dogs were trained for war, and nearly 3,000 dogs were sent overseas. Dogs proved to be an invaluable resource in the Pacific and on the home front. When the dogs were recruited, owners were promised return of their dogs if they survived the war. That promise was difficult to fulfill. The U.S. military did not anticipate the thousands of hours of retraining needed and the cost that such a promise would require. But through the work of Lt. William Putney and Maj. Harold C. Gors, dogs were given demilitarization training and sent home.

Putney was appalled to learn that, before he could object, several marine war dogs had been euthanized in the Pacific. He believed that with proper demilitarization all the dogs could return to a civilian life. He therefore refused to sign a single dog's death certificate until he was certain that every effort had been made to retrain the dog. Of the 559 marine war dogs living at the end of the war, 540 were returned to civilian life. Of the 19 others, only four were unable to be re-

were taken to ensure dogs had clean, fresh water every day and that their water bowls were boiled at least once a month to prevent the growth of harmful bacteria.

One problem encountered by the 2nd and 3rd U.S. Marine Corps War Dog Platoons was a posterior paralysis of many of the dogs. At first, this paralysis was a mystery to Lieutenant Putney. Although he was a civilian veterinarian, his assignment to a war-dog platoon was not as its veterinarian, but as a line officer. He led 110 marines and 72 dogs from Camps Lejeune and Pendleton to Guadalcanal and Guam, setting up field hospitals along the way to treat the dogs. He determined that supplementing the dogs' diets with frozen fish was causing a B-vitamin deficiency, which led to paralysis. He ordered that the dogs no longer be fed the fish and requested supplies of B-1 vitamins.

The medical attention required by war-dog platoons was not limited to treatment of com-

trained. The other 15 were euthanized because of health problems.

Dogs for Defense, which stopped procuring dogs in March 1945, spoke vehemently for the return of war dogs to civilian life. In *Dogs for Defense: American Animals in the Second World War*, the organization stated, "We feel that the place for a K-9 veteran is in a home and not in some kennel or an army post. To say that a dog should be kept confined to a kennel, robbed of the pleasure of companionship only to be found in a home, seemed to us just like arguing that the soldier for whom no job is in sight should be kept in uniform indefinitely." Many Americans were ready and willing to take the K-9 war heroes into their homes. In 1945, Congress passed a bill allowing dog handlers to adopt their dogs if the original owners did not want them. The deep personal connection that developed between the dogs and their handlers was an unanticipated aspect of the war-dog training program.

The intense training, stress of combat, and reliance on each other for survival created a strong bond between dog and handler. The handler and other soldiers depended on the dog to protect them and to alert to an enemy, and the dog

A marine corps German shepherd is comforted by his partner while being x-rayed. The dog, shot by a Japanese sniper on Bougainville, died of his injuries. *National Archives photo.*

Scout dogs of the army's Marauder Infantry pose with their handlers in Burma. *National Archives photo.*

depended on its handler to feed him, give him water, and generally care for him. Allowing handlers and their dogs to remain together when possible helped both the dog and the soldier adjust to their return to civilian life. Those dogs that did go back to their original owners all recognized their civilian families even though they had been gone for up to three years. There were no reports of demilitarized war dogs attacking or injuring people after their return home.

In World War II, the war-dog training program was new, untested, and groundbreaking. The insights and knowledge gained from large-scale training and intense combat experience would allow the K-9 Corps to flourish in postwar America. The success of dogs in military, police, and humanitarian roles today owes much to those dogs of World War II that embarked on a journey to unknown territory and became warriors and heroes.

Smoky. *Photo copyright © William A. Wynne, used courtesy William A. Wynne.*

Smoky was a Yorkshire terrier that belonged to William Wynne of Ohio. Wynne adopted her while serving with the 5th Air Force in the Pacific theater. Smoky was found in a foxhole and at first was assumed to be a Japanese soldier's dog. But when she did not respond to commands in Japanese or English, Wynne adopted her and began training her to become quite the show dog.

Smoky performed numerous tricks but also flew along on twelve missions, usually riding in a soldier's pack. She survived along with Wynne in the dense jungle on C-rations and Spam. She endured 150 air raids and even a typhoon.

Smoky became a true war dog when she used her diminutive size to run through a culvert under a runway. Engineers were building a crucial airfield in Luzon. The Signal Corps needed to run telegraph wire through a seventy-foot pipe that was eight inches in diameter. Smoky's extensive training and calls from Wynne brought her through the tunnel with the wire attached to her collar.

What would have taken troops three days and caused serious operational delays was accomplished by Smoky with only a few minutes' work. After the war, Smoky came home with Wynne and continued to perform her tricks. She was featured on television and in magazine articles across the United States.

Rocky was a marine Devil Dog handled by PFC Marvin Corff. Rocky and Corff worked in Guam's mop-up campaign. They went on more than fifty patrols, sometimes staying out for over two weeks at a time. On one patrol, Corff killed four Japanese soldiers after Rocky alerted to them. Corff earned a Silver Star for his bravery. After the war, Rocky was demilitarized and sent home to his original owner. Corff visited Rocky occasionally, but at one point he wrote to his commanding officer, Lt. William Putney, "He [Rocky] was glad to see me and would obey my commands, but I felt it best not to go back anymore because my visits were making it difficult for him to adjust to his new civilian life."

Members of a machine-gun crew load a pack mule with a .30 caliber gun and ammunition for the long trek up a mountain pass in Italy in 1943. *Gift of Regan Forrester, 2002.337.306.*

2. The Army Mule

Mules are often looked down upon because of their purportedly stubborn and abject nature, but the phrase "tough as a government mule" still rings true and emotes the hardworking qualities of this widely used beast. Despite their commonly perceived faults, mules have always been an important part of the U.S. Army, even within the fully mechanized army of World War II. Mules' sturdy nature and surefootedness were vital on rugged terrain impassable by military vehicles. They also required less grain than horses and made a much more dependable work animal. Contrary to widespread belief, mules are intelligent animals. Their intelligence helps them recognize their own limits of strength and endurance. This quality is sometimes read as stubbornness, but unlike horses, mules will not work themselves to death.

Mules have always fallen under the army's Quartermaster Department, which in turn supplies them to military units in need. Mules were introduced into the U.S. Army in the mid 1830s. The first few were procured during the Indian campaigns of the Midwest and later for the fighting in Texas and Mexico. In 1860, one year before the start of the American Civil War, Union quar-

termasters alone purchased over 75,000 mules for their growing army. The American army of World War I used mules by the hundreds of thousands. A young Lt. Lucian Truscott, later to be famous for his use of mules in Italy during World War II, especially campaigned for their use. American mules were shipped to Great Britain and France starting in 1917, and in total nearly 30,000 mules were shipped to Europe by the end of World War I. A great number of these animals died from American unpreparedness and general ignorance on the part of the animals' handlers concerning their care during shipment and combat conditions. So many horses and mules died during World War I that the dead animals were famously sold to Paris butchers, becoming standard French fare. Mule meat also supplemented British civilians during food shortages at the end of the war.

During the period following World War I, the U.S. Army kept nearly 80,000 mules; however, the military was turning decisively toward total mechanization, expecting to rely on aircraft and motorized, mobile units for the future of the army. Therefore, in 1940, only four regiments with mules still existed. The army realized early in World War II that many more mules would

Muleskinners attached to the 2nd Battalion, 475th Infantry Regiment, Mars Task Force, stripped down to their bare skin to lead mules through the swift river that impeded their progress to Bhamo, Burma. *National Archives photo.*

be needed. In their book *The United States Army in World War II . . . The Quartermaster Corps: Organization, Supply, and Services,* Erna Risch and Giltsler L. Kieffer note that the U.S. Army purchased more horses than mules from the start of the war until 1943. In that year, the army acquired more than 10,000 mules and only four horses. No other horses were purchased for the remainder of the war, but over 14,000 additional mules were, indicating the importance of these animals even within a mechanized army.

During World War II, mules worked around the world, for both Allied and Axis armies. Mules served units in Africa and in higher numbers in Italy, but formed a decisive backbone of support and mobilization in the China-Burma-India (CBI)

theater. This theater was one of the most geographically challenging environments in which soldiers saw combat during World War II. It was a place where mules proved themselves even more versatile than the jeep.

At times during the harsh North African, Italian, and Burmese campaigns, mules were the only source of supply for soldiers. Pack-mule units were created in anticipation of the dire need for supplies by troops who could not be reached by any other means of transportation. The mules were best utilized when supplies were carried by vehicle until wheels and tracks could no longer cross the terrain. Then the mules took over for the short and rugged distances to the front line. Mules could walk nearly twenty miles

Pack mules of the Mars Task Force traveling in nearly single file through mountainous terrain in Burma. *Gift of John H. Tate II, 2010.502.010.*

in one day on normal terrain and up to ten miles in mountainous terrain. They were expected to walk anywhere a man could walk without using his hands for support.

The mission of pack transportation, as stated in the 1944 army manual on that subject, is "to transport loads on the backs of animals over terrain, which is difficult for or impassable to wheeled, or track laying vehicles. Its success depends largely upon the careful selection and training of personnel and pack animals." The use of correct packing and marching techniques was essential for the success of the unit. The pack train's disadvantage was its slow speed, sometimes not exceeding five miles per day in the worst conditions.

Three distinct types of pack transportation were used in the U.S. Army during World War II. Cargo pack trains were operated by the Quartermaster Corps in support of artillery, infantry, and engineer units. Their loads were generally bulky and heavy and were secured to packsaddles by ropes. Artillery combat pack units provided another type of pack transportation. Animals in these units carried the heaviest loads, including broken-down howitzer pieces (such as the 75 mm pack howitzer), large instruments, communication equipment, and ammunition. These loads were secured to the saddles with special arches, adapters, and hangers to support and contain them. The third type of pack transportation was the horse cavalry, which carried lighter and less bulky loads. These loads were light enough to allow the animals to trot or gallop without destroying the integrity of the packed load. The first two types of pack transportation utilized mules only, while the third used horses or mules.

According to the manual mentioned above, "A pack mule should be from 14 and three quarter hands to 15 and one half hands in height and weigh from 1,000 to 1,200 pounds. He should be compact, stockily built, and have a short neck; short, straight, strong, and well-muscled back and loins; low withers and croup; large barrel

African American soldiers riding and leading mules through trails in Burma. *Gift of John H. Tate II, 2010.502.012.*

with deep girth; straight, strong legs; and short pasterns and good feet." The mules were also selected for their composure, quietness, and calmness—traits that were important when hundreds of mules were moving together through narrow pathways in intimidating jungles.

The training of mules was imperative to the entire unit's success. All pack-transportation units were trained on the terrain in which they were expected to operate in future campaigns. Many mules were trained in the Rocky Mountains at Camp Carson, Colorado, and in the mountainous areas around Fort Ord, California. The successful mobility of a pack train depended largely on the selection and training of gentle and

manageable mules. Also critical was the ability of the muleskinners to care for and correctly pack the animals so as to obtain the maximum payload without detriment to the animals' health.

Training in pack units consisted of physical conditioning of both men and mules. The soldiers' training included extensive practice in packing all types of loads and the marching of the animals under these full loads over all types of terrain. According to the army pack-transportation manual, "Good march discipline, a thorough knowledge of pack transportation, and careful supervision of the march are essential to success." Training was implemented by patient, persistent, and positive methods of instruction. The pack train as a whole

Wire crew from the 63rd Signal Battalion checking communication wire while a convoy of mules led by Italian muleskinners goes by. The mules are hauling rations to outfits not possible to reach by truck. *Gift of William F. Caddell Jr., 2007.048.533.*

to become familiar with the smell of gasoline and the sound of engines. They were also led among low-flying aircraft and near gunfire. Through this conditioning, the animals learned that the noises and events around them would not hurt them. As a result, they would remain calm in the field. Pack-unit soldiers excelled at the patience needed to persuade and encourage these animals. Mules were worked through intensive training programs before being shipped overseas. The most well trained mule of the unit was deemed the bell mare, or the lead pack mule. She wore a special bell around her neck to alert those around her to her presence. All mules were trained to follow the bell mare through any kind of conditions.

The U.S. Army used the Phillips cargo packsaddle. This saddle was used for all pack artillery loads, all pack-train loads, and the heavier infantry-weapon cargo loads. It weighed seventy-two pounds without a load. The saddle consisted of a metal frame with padding, breeching, cinches, and a woven pad; with all of its attachments the saddle could weigh up to ninety-five pounds, again without a load. The frame was specially designed to support heavy top loads. A smaller version of this saddle was developed later in the war for smaller Chinese mules and was called the Phillips cavalry packsaddle, modified (China Special). Packsaddles were cleaned daily to withstand the elements, and were fully dismantled and cleaned once per week. As much as 250 pounds of cargo could be packed onto these saddles. Smooth-surfaced items were often wrapped in canvas or burlap sacks to better secure them to the load with rope. Three hundred mules carrying three hundred pounds each meant that one pack unit could carry forty-five tons.

There were four positions for individual soldiers within a pack unit: packer, cargador, packmaster, and train commander. The packer was an understudy to the cargador and had to work

greatly benefited from the gentleness and passivity of a well-trained herd when moving forward during combat.

The U.S. Army selected muleskinners based on their knowledge and lack of fear of large animals. Mule handlers were expected to be patient, kind, and firm. They were instructed to train the mules with positive reinforcement, rewarding the mule with petting and hand feeding. Sticks, switches, or other items instilling fear were prohibited. All mules were trained to be ridden, to be led, to stand quietly, to walk and stand fully packed, to move in a herd, to swim, and, finally, to be immersed in the sounds of battle. Battle inoculation was achieved by working with the mules around motor parks, allowing the animals

American soldiers killed in mountain fighting were transported from ridges and summits by mules to vehicle stations. Here, a dead soldier in Italy on a litter is being wrapped in a blanket before being loaded onto the mule. *Gift of Regan Forrester, 2002.337.317.*

especially well with animals. His specific duties were training and saddling mules, riding them, caring for them in the field, caring for the saddle, preparing cargo in loads for packing, and later removing the loads from the animal. The cargador (a somewhat antiquated term meaning "one who carries") performed many of the same duties of the packer, but was also the saddler and was responsible for all saddle repairs. The cargador's specific duties included assigning pack mules and equipment to the packers, instructing packers, assigning saddles and loads at the beginning of each day, matching up cargo to make balanced payloads on the mules, ensuring quiet and gentle treatment of pack mules, removing the saddles of all mules during bivouac, and keeping a record of all cargo and equipment under his care.

The packmaster was responsible for the presence, care, and maintenance of all pack equipment and animals. He rode along the entire column in order to check all loads and observe the condition of his men and animals. The packmaster's specific duties included supervising all packing, especially making sure that loads were properly packed to avoid injury to the animals' backs and ordering readjustment of loads whenever necessary; ensuring the overall proper care of pack animals at all times; checking the mules for injuries when the packsaddles were removed; ensuring that all breakage or damage to packsaddles was repaired; and checking animals on the march for signs of distress or weakness and, if necessary, relieving them of their loads. The train commander was the officer placed in charge of the column. His specific duties included taking all responsibility for the conduct of the train, enforcing strict care and conditioning of the mules, enforcing measures for proper cover, concealment, and protection against surprise attacks by enemy air or ground forces, and all other duties of a commanding officer in the field.

In the field, mules were led in a column. The

Mules tied up along a picket line in a clearing set up for camp in Burma. *Gift of John H. Tate II, 2010.502.016.*

column was to stay at a constant pace, with the animals not allowed to increase speed through trotting or to jump over obstacles, as these motions could displace the load and injure the mule. Usually the packers walked ahead of the animals, helping to lead the column and maintain a constant pace, but over rugged terrain the muleskinner (generally the lower of the aforementioned positions) would fall behind the animal to allow it to see most of its surroundings and maintain its surefootedness. All men not assigned to a mule walked behind the animals to keep an eye on their loads and saddles, making sure they had not slipped or become uneven. The army field manual on pack transportation clearly states,

"Under no circumstances will personnel hold on to the saddle, breeching, or animal's tail to assist themselves in walking," but this was often ignored. Many times on a long upward slope, the mules not only carried the weight of the loads, but also helped pull up the men behind them who were holding onto their tails.

Once the column had completed its day's march, the pack-train commander advanced to select a bivouac area large enough for all of the men, mules, cargo, and saddles. Upon the column's arrival, the mules were tied to a picket line and their loads and saddles removed. The mules were then released to roll on the ground, thereby resting and massaging their back muscles. Later,

Mule pack train on the way to the Italian front passing a wrecked German assault gun lying by the roadside. *Gift of Regan Forrester, 2002.337.228.*

the animals were watered and groomed thoroughly. At night, the mules, the unit's equipment, and all cargo were arranged systematically in the bivouac so they could be loaded and moved in a moment's notice.

MULES IN NORTH AFRICA

Mules were used in North Africa, but not in the more efficient and careful way that they would be used later in the war. Instead of shipping trained mules overseas from the United States, the American army scrambled to find mules and donkeys to rent or buy from local North Africans. The muleskinners also found saddles and food for the animals locally. But even these small, untrained

mules were effective at bringing supplies to Allied troops through deserts and other harsh terrains until engineers could build appropriate roads.

MULES IN ITALY

The same problems encountered in North Africa occurred in Sicily. Mules were purchased, rented, or commandeered from local Italians. The U.S. Army still did not grasp the importance of training for the animals. Conditions were terrible for mules in Italy. There were very few veterinarians and inadequate food and water. In addition, the general policy was to replace sick or injured animals rather than give them the necessary care to return them to health. These early mule units

Advancing infantrymen of an Algerian division look at their fallen buddy and his pack mule killed by a German shell near Esperia, Italy. *Gift of Regan Forrester, 2002.337.541.*

were hodgepodge, whereas in the later years of the war, complete and organized mule trains would develop in the China-Burma-India theater.

Mules were used in Sicily to support troops of the 3rd Infantry Division as provisional pack-mule trains under the aforementioned General Truscott. Truscott had used mules in North Africa, where he acquired more than four hundred of them along with one thousand horses for support. Mule trains were often used in Sicily to deliver ammunition from the amphibious forces on the beach to the artillery battalions in the mountains.

The U.S. Fifth Army in Italy also received small but important reinforcements necessary in mountain warfare; two battalions of U.S. pack artillery (75 mm pack howitzers) and two Italian pack-mule companies. As stated by Emmett Essin in *Shavetails and Bell Sharps*, "The Fifth Army needed artillery set up where only mules could put it." This would continue to be true all over the world. Unfortunately, American mules did not

have their chance to shine in this campaign, as they were never prioritized to cross the Atlantic with other supplies. Nonetheless, the army realized that these animals were necessary in specific environments, even as part of a mechanized army.

MULES IN THE PACIFIC

Pack mules were used in the Pacific theater, but not extensively and not to any great effect. Tropical diseases and a wet climate affected the mules just as it did men. The lack of any natural fodder was also an insurmountable problem in jungle climates.

THE CHINA-BURMA-INDIA (CBI) THEATER AND THE MARS TASK FORCE

The most famous pack-mule unit in the CBI, and probably World War II, was the Mars Task Force, a successful and self-sufficient military unit. It was self-sufficient because of the cargo loads

Hiram Boone, a member of the Mars Task Force, riding his mule Chick while leading another in Burma. *Gift of Hiram Vance Boone, 2006.102.096.*

supported by the 612th and 613th Field Artillery Battalions (Pack) and the traveling medical, quartermaster, and veterinary units. The Mars Task Force was the ultimate proof of animals' importance in a mechanized army in cases where mobility in rough terrain was more important than speed.

The 5332nd Brigade (Provisional), or Mars Task Force, was the second of two American long-range penetration units that employed mules and fought behind Japanese lines in the jungles of Burma, today's Myanmar. The task force was created in July 1944 with components of its predecessor, Merrill's Marauders (who became the 475th Infantry Regiment), and the 124th Cavalry Regiment. Its job was to function behind Japanese lines in the deep jungles and mountains of

southeast Asia. From any vantage, this terrain was intimidating. It was also impossible for most motorized vehicles to cross. Strong, sure-footed mules were needed to carry artillery on mountain trails, sometimes in single file. The men of the Mars Task Force were so far behind enemy lines that they only received air-dropped supplies and relied solely on small liaison planes for the evacuation of wounded and sick along the treacherous routes. Except for these planes, mechanized transportation was not feasible; therefore, mules became the force's only reliable means for the movement of supplies.

The Mars Task Force and its predecessor, Merrill's Marauders, were charged with protecting China's supply routes. This was an important objective for the United States, as America was

Members of the 612th Field Artillery Battalion (Pack), Mars Task Force, leading loaded mules across a river in Burma. *Gift of Hiram Vance Boone, 2002.200.*

determined to keep China's soldiers engaged with the Japanese. Specifically, the Mars Task Force was fighting in Burma to protect the Ledo Road, a bypass from Allied-controlled Ledo, India, past the Japanese-controlled part of the Burma Road. Key to their success—and something Merrill's Marauders before them did not have—was the Marsmen's self-sufficiency through attached supporting pack units traveling with them.

The two pack-mule Field Artillery Battalions (FABs), the 612th and 613th FABs, arrived in India in late 1944. Soldiers forming these units had trained extensively with mules at Camp Carson in the Colorado Rocky Mountains. The mules, originally from Missouri, crossed two oceans to reach India. Most ships, sailing to India via Los Angeles or New Orleans, traveled with 200–300

mules per vessel and averaged two months at sea. The ratio of mules to men in the Mars Task Force FABs was almost 1 to 1, the 613th FAB entering combat with 347 mules and 445 men. In total, the Mars Task Force numbered about 7,000 men with their supplies, supported by 3,000 mules. Along with the indispensable mules, each battalion had a contingent of Kachin soldiers (native Burmese working with the Office of Strategic Services as intelligence and reconnaissance forces), war dogs, veterinarians, Nisei (Japanese-American) translators, and Chinese interpreters.

The majority of the Mars Task Force moved through the mountainous jungles in a column consisting of cavalry platoons (without mules or horses), followed by the mules and their mule-skinners, with war dogs interspersed through-

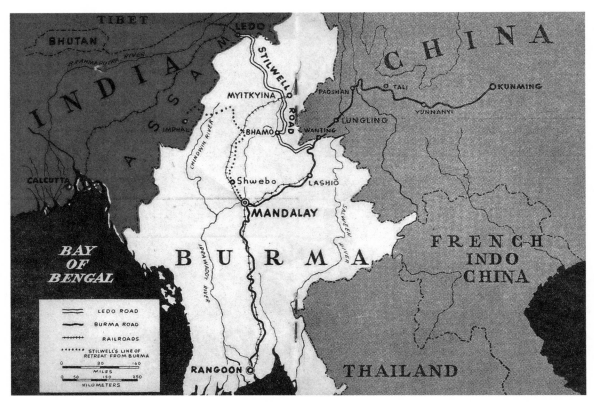

Map of the China-Burma-India theater as it looked during World War II. From the booklet *Stilwell Road: Story of the Ledo Lifeline.* *Gift of Gerald F. Vessely, 2009.563.172.*

Kachin guide killed in the Battle of Myitkyina in Burma in 1944. *Gift of Greg Anderson, 2003.171.*

Men of the 612th Field Artillery Battalion load pack mules with 75 mm shells while parachutes fall with more ammunition and supplies. From *Marsmen in Burma*, by John Randolph. *Gift of Hiram Vance Boone, 2002.210.001.*

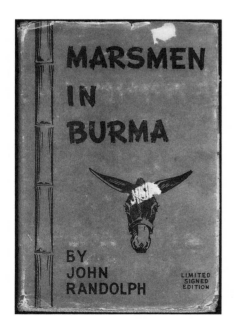

Cover of *Marsmen in Burma*, by John Randolph. *Gift of Hiram Vance Boone, 2002.210.001.*

out. The schedule consisted of fifty minutes of marching followed by ten minutes of rest. This column would sometimes take, from beginning to end, an hour and a half to cross the same mark, or even longer when the column was forced to march single file. Supplies were air-dropped every three days, and when convenient, a rest day would coincide with the supply drop to allow for medical and veterinary attention. One rest day was allowed per week. Rations for soldiers and grain for mules arrived through air drop. Six to eight burlap bags, each with fifty pounds of grain, were dropped without parachutes, a sometimes dangerous way to deliver food to those below. Army grain was a mixture of barley, oats, and salt, rationed at ten pounds per mule per day.

In addition to artillery, the FAB mules carried supplies and weaponry for other members of the task force. Their loads contained anything from ammunition to oats. Each animal was loaded with as many supplies as possible without exceeding the animal's weight limit. Loads constantly varied as rations were consumed or new supplies added. This often resulted in an oddly mixed and strangely attached load. A usual day of marching included muleskinners moving up and down mule columns adjusting straps as uneven or overheavy loads both physically exhausted the animals and hurt them by scraping skin and creating sores. In *Marsmen in Burma*, John Randolph tells a story of an unbalanced load falling loose and off the saddle, scaring a mule into a sprint with a muleskinner dragging behind it in an effort to save the animal and its precious cargo.

Mules were also tested in the jungles for use as nonmechanized ambulances. The idea was to equip them with a litter to transport wounded men out of the jungle. Various mules were tested to see which would endure carrying a man and litter, as each time the animal lifted its head, its neck would hit the litter. When a tolerant mule was found, a GI would volunteer to ride in the litter to test the experience of the wounded. However, as the volunteers often suffered injuries from the jostling and bouncing, the idea was discarded.

The constant marching was hard for the men and animals, but they often rallied each other. During the ten-minute breaks, the mules were usually offered oats or grain from a nosebag around their necks as the men enjoyed a D-ration chocolate bar. Often muleskinners would fetch water for their mules in their helmets, toting it from a nearby creek. Nearness to water at nightfall was a necessity for the mules.

The 75 mm M1A1 pack howitzer was the largest artillery piece used by the Mars Task Force. It was also the largest piece of artillery that could be broken down and carried solely on the backs of mules. The need for artillery was a shortcoming identified by Merrill's Marauders, who were previously outgunned by the Japanese. This howitzer was designed for quick assembly and disassembly and could be broken down for individual pack-mule loads. The 612th and 613th FABs had a headquarters and service battery and three gun batteries; the gun batteries had four 75 mm pack howitzers each, for a total of twenty-four howitzers supporting the Mars Task Force. Each gun had its own crew, plus a crew of muleskinners tasked with packing and unloading the weapons during combat and every night.

After six months of jungle marching in late 1944 and early 1945, the task force defeated the Japanese at Tonkwa and the battle of Loi-kang Ridge. By firing twelve thousand rounds of ammunition, all carried by mules, the Mars Task Force pushed the Japanese out of northern Burma. With no remaining combat missions in Burma, the unit was to travel with its mules to China, to advise and train the Nationalist Chinese army. Most of the Marsmen were flown into

Army mule in New Guinea equipped with a specially designed litter for carrying wounded men out of the jungle. *The National WWII Museum, 2010.122.001.*

A member of the Mars Task Force fires his 75 mm pack howitzer in the jungles of Burma. *Gift of Minda Cutcher, 2003.187.*

Veterinarians testing for disease outside of Kunming, China, in 1945. *Gift of Hiram Vance Boone, 2002.210.011.*

China, but the three thousand mules were moved overland. Two thousand mules were handed over to the Chinese army's pack artillery units; but one thousand did not survive the war. The main cause of death was surra, an insect-borne parasitic blood disease found in Asia.

HIRAM BOONE, 612TH FAB

Born in 1921 in Marion, Virginia, Hiram Boone went to work at a gunpowder company for the war effort after graduating from high school. He then worked at the Sunflower Ordnance Plant in Lawrence, Kansas, until the age of twenty-two, when he received a bonus from the power company to join the service. He was inducted on September 23, 1943. Boone was posted at Fort Sill, Oklahoma, for artillery training, where he took basic training and worked specifically with the 75 mm pack howitzer and mules. At Camp Gruber, Oklahoma, Boone became a member of the 612th FAB, assigned to the Headquarters and Service battery. Here Boone again trained with the 75

mm pack howitzer and mules. He then trained at Camp Carson, Colorado, to prepare for the mountains of Burma, although his battalion had no idea yet where they would be fighting. They trained with the mules in the rapid unpacking of artillery and then piecing it together for combat. According to Boone, "A gun could be unloaded in a matter of minutes and be in firing position."

Boone was shipped overseas out of New Orleans, Louisiana, after a one-month stay at Jackson Barracks, the mules having been held at Camp Plauche, Louisiana. Boone set sail for Calcutta with three hundred mules on the SS *Cyrus W. Fields*, a ship specifically equipped to hold that many animals below deck. The ship first sailed around the Florida keys to reach Norfolk, Virginia, where a convoy was formed to cross the Atlantic. The 612th FAB and their mules traveled sixty-three days through the Atlantic, the Mediterranean, the Suez Canal, and the Red Sea, finally reaching the Indian Ocean and Calcutta on September 23, 1944. There was no training aboardship, just care and maintenance of the

S. S. Cyrus W. Field
July '44
22th. Loaded on ship
1:19 P.M. Circuled in
harbor until 5:00 P.M.
getting instruments set.
23rd. All is well. What
a ride.
24th. Exercising Mule on
top deck, he stepped on
left foot, nothing serious.
Wrote first letter to
"Maple" + Mom.
25th. Ocean Very Calm
Nice sailing.
26th. What a Contrast
in the ocean to-day and

Portrait of Hiram Vance Boone, 612th Field Artillery Battalion (Pack), 5332nd Brigade (Provisional), Mars Task Force. *Gift of Hiram Vance Boone, 2006.102.018.*

Page from Boone's journal during his time aboard the SS *Cyrus W. Field,* the ship that transported mules from the United States to Calcutta, India. Here he discusses exercising the animals on deck. *Gift of Hiram Vance Boone, 2006.102.140.*

Boone standing next to the flag of the 612th Field Artillery Battalion (Pack) headquarters in China. *Gift of Hiram Vance Boone, 2002.210.021.*

three hundred mules, whose waste was dumped off the ship at night to prevent the Germans from tracking the convoy. The mules were kept below the decks, but were taken up once a day to exercise. Their stalls below deck were cleaned each night.

When the 612th FAB moved out of Calcutta in late September 1944, the animals were taken by railroad car to Camp Landis in northern Burma. At Camp Landis, the 612th FAB trained with the 475th Infantry Regiment, the regiment they specifically supported. The 613th FAB trained with the 124th Cavalry Regiment. Here both battalions trained with live fire.

Loads were not to exceed three hundred pounds per mule. Under this weight limit, it took nine mules to carry one disassembled 75 mm pack howitzer. The 612th FAB mules also carried ammunition along with all other supplies.

Boone's job in the field was to collect ammunition, food, and other supplies from air drops as already described. He had to be at a certain location on a given date to reach the dropped goods before the Japanese found them. All supplies were then loaded on the mule packs to be carried out of the drop zone. Artillery, ammunition (including 75 mm artillery rounds), and rations were air-dropped by parachute, but mule feed was free-dropped because the bags were packaged loosely and would not burst on impact. All mule feed was shipped from the United States and then air-dropped from C-47s. Boone would locate the clearing for the drop, collect the supplies, and load everything onto the mules.

Boone's personal riding mount, his mule Chick, traveled with him from the beginning of his journey all the way to China. After Chick was assigned to Boone at Camp Landis, Boone cared for and groomed the animal every day, in addition to his other duties. He said of the Mars mules in his oral history, recorded in 2006, "They're smart, much smarter than horses, they will not over-drink, they will not overeat, they will not overwork, they are superior in footage in rough terrain to a horse and they are actually smarter than a horse." Boone recalls once seeing a mule fall off a mountain cliff. Some of the men located the supplies and carted them up, leaving the mule for dead. Three days later, the mule found its way back to the 612th FAB camp and rejoined the unit.

Boone and the other members of this long-range penetration unit marched and marched. The longest march made by the 612th FAB was thirty-six hours, with only three hours' rest. Walking at elevations of 8,000 feet with little rest was hard for both the animals and the men.

Hiram Boone's mule Chick, "the best mule in the Army," according to Boone, in China. Note Boone's camera case attached to the saddle's pommel. *Gift of Hiram Vance Boone, 2002.210.022.*

The 612th FAB and the 475th Infantry Regiment had their first skirmish with the Japanese in Tonkwa. During the engagement, the men with pack howitzers tried to dig in and use some sort of camouflage. Boone remembers Chinese soldiers fighting alongside the Marsmen. After Tonkwa, the task force resumed its duty as a long-range penetration unit. Boone reasoned that a smaller brigade was used because it was easier to supply, especially solely by air-drop, than a larger division. He says of the air drops, "We had what we needed, I guess, but no excess."

Boone describes the 612th FAB as sort of a harassing unit—one attempting to fool the Japanese as to their actual numbers and where they were positioned. They would often hit a Japanese-held area, then retreat to do it again from another location. Their goal was to keep the Japanese off guard. Namhpakka was the fiercest battle fought by the 612th FAB, at the end of their campaign,

at the juncture of the Burma and Ledo Roads. The Japanese had mechanized equipment on the Burma Road and could fire at the Marsmen, but the Marsmen, who were obviously not mechanized, had to get their 75 mm howitzers high enough to fire down onto the Burma Road to destroy the Japanese equipment below—an objective they achieved. The Marsmen relied solely on their mules for artillery support, a component absolutely necessary to pushing back the Japanese.

When the 612th FAB's combat actions in Namhpakka ended, the unit was ordered to provide the Chinese army with the mules the Americans no longer needed. Unfortunately, many of the mules contracted the disease surra, which would eventually be fatal to the animals. The mules were tested for disease outside of Kunming, China. Boone and the rest of the 612th FAB felt the humane way to treat the mules would be to destroy them before the disease could kill

Members of the 612th Field Artillery Battalion (Pack), riding and leading pack mules with full packs along the Burma Road. *Gift of Hiram Vance Boone, 2002.210.010.*

A member of the 612th Field Artillery Battalion (Pack) shooting mules outside of Kunming, where several hundred were destroyed after found to be diseased. *Gift of Hiram Vance Boone, 2002.210.012.*

them. Sadly, even Chick caught the fatal disease and had to be destroyed after many months of loyal and dedicated service to Boone and the Marsmen. Lieutenant Shortt of the 612th FAB shot many of the mules outside Kunming. The mules were shot on the side of a cliff so that they would fall into the ravine. Engineers blasted the surrounding hills to cover the animals' bodies.

After the breakup of the Mars Task Force, Boone was assigned to the 272nd Military Police Company in Kunming. Boone left China on December 8, 1945, returning to the United States on a C-54 by flying the hump to Calcutta and then taking the transport ship *SS General J. R. Brooke* home. He arrived January 3, 1946, and was discharged on the ninth. Boone kept in touch with members of pack-mule artillery battalions through the Mountain Artillery Association, which took its members from the 612th and 613th FABs. Boone ended his oral history with this thought, "I did want to praise this mule, and I frankly think that mules and other animals did not receive and have not received the recognition they are entitled to, because they all did pay the supreme sacrifice."

An army pigeon that distinguished itself by carrying the first message by pigeon service in Italy. *Gift of Regan Forrester, 2002.337.283.*

3. Pigeons

Homing pigeons, one of the oldest means of long-distance communication, were widely used during World War II. These pigeons are a specific type of domestic pigeon derived from the rock pigeon, and are unlike feral pigeons that roam most cities. The earliest documented use of pigeons for communication was by the Romans two thousand years ago. Their ability to carry important messages has not diminished in the long period of time since. Even before Japan's attack on Pearl Harbor in December 1941, the American military had begun ramping up its communications programs within the army's Signal Corps branch. During the war, carrier pigeons were used in almost every theater, by almost every army, both Axis and Allied.

About a dozen American pigeon units were activated during World War II. These included the 283rd Signal Pigeon Company, the 829th Signal Pigeon Service Company, the 829th Signal Pigeon Replacement Service Company, and the 1306th and 1310th Signal Pigeon Companies (Aviation), the last two belonging to the army air forces. None of these units went overseas. The signal pigeon companies that did go abroad were the 277th, the 278th, the 279th, the 280th, the 281st, the 282nd, the 284th, and the 285th. In a global positioning, the 277th, 278th, 282nd, and 284th went to Europe while the 279th saw combat in the Central Pacific, the 280th in both the European and CBI theaters, and the 281st in the Southwest Pacific. During World War II, the army's Signal Corps had over 3,000 soldiers and 150 officers assigned to the U.S. Military Pigeon Service. They cared for more than 54,000 military pigeons, 36,000 of which were deployed overseas. The pigeons were used in every combat theater and saw service with ground troops, on submarines, in bombers, and within the intelligence service. In an astounding rate of success, Signal Corps soldiers received more than 90 percent of army messages sent by pigeon.

Pigeons often had to accomplish their missions under difficult conditions: bad weather, night flying, different home lofts, bullet showers, and attack from enemy birds of prey. Thousands of Allied soldiers, airmen, and sailors owe their lives to these small animals and the pigeoneers who trained them to deliver messages when all other methods failed. We know that the Axis forces were also interested in pigeons, as Sgt. Charles Heitzman, a pigeon fancier of interna-

U.S. soldier placing a pigeon in a combat pigeon carrier. *Courtesy Hayes Collection, Holt-Atherton Special Collections, University of the Pacific Library.*

tional renown who became a leading figure in the Signal Corps pigeon unit, was approached by Japanese men looking for the best messenger pigeons in the United States. This being some time before Pearl Harbor, Heitzman sold the men some of his best pigeons. Later, realizing what he had done only spurred Heitzman's desire to breed and train smarter and stronger pigeons than his earlier birds.

In 1943, pigeons, as a means of communication, formed less than one percent of the Signal Corps' services. However, even as the army moved toward near-total mechanization, these birds remained valuable to all branches of the military, as they were considered an undetectable method of communication. They were utilized especially when other means of sending messages had failed or were not feasible, such as times of radio failure or when troops were under orders of radio silence. Pigeons were also an important part of war communication in places where stringing wire was impossible, such as Guadal-

canal and other Pacific jungle islands. Pigeons were equally important for paratroopers—an innovation of World War II for placing soldiers behind enemy lines—who frequently had little or no radio communications from their drop zones. Pigeons brought news about the drop zone back to headquarters swiftly and without revealing the location of the soldiers. Pigeons were also dropped via specially made parachutes, or inside bamboo containers equipped with parachutes, to patrols operating behind enemy lines. The containers and parachutes were necessary so that the pigeons would not immediately fly home when released. The soldiers collected the pigeons and attached messages to them before sending them home with the communication. Air crews also carried pigeons in case they had to ditch their plane. The crew would release the bird with their coordinates to send for help, and as a result many pilots owe their lives to a pigeon.

The U.S. Army specified that pigeons were to be used as a means of communication only as a

Diagram taken from the technical manual *The Homing Pigeon*, TM 11-410, showing the message capsule correctly attached to a pigeon's leg. *The National World War Museum, 2008.273.*

An American armored outfit's request for help upon all other communication failure. This message was successfully delivered by carrier pigeon. *Courtesy Hayes Collection, Holt-Atherton Special Collections, University of the Pacific Library.*

last resort. Pigeons were valuable as forward elements when telephone lines and wireless technology were hampered by the unexpectedness of war. One of the greatest advantages of using pigeons on the front lines (or in enemy territory, as in the case of paratroopers) was that the soldier needed no special training when releasing the bird. He could simply write a message, attach the capsule to the bird's leg, and let go. The bird's advanced training and natural abilities gave the front-line soldier confidence that the bird, and therefore the message, would be successfully received.

By 1943, pigeons were a regular extension of a bomber aircraft's equipment. The hope was that the birds would escape damaged aircraft with the crew and return their coordinates to the Signal Corps, who would then alert rescue crews. The pigeons carried thin paper messages placed in a tiny container attached to the leg. The birds could also carry slightly heavier messages, using cigar-size capsules attached to their backs, but

this did not occur frequently. Very few messages were encoded, as pigeons were so dependable at returning to their home lofts, soldiers did not worry about them falling into enemy hands.

HOW HOMING PIGEONS WORK

Although homing pigeons' talents are very well known, a greater understanding of their abilities is necessary to appreciate their successful use by the military. The genius of using carrier, or homing, pigeons is their inherent ability to return to their home loft, no matter its geographic location. The bird must be trained very early in its life, and the home loft also must be established early in the pigeon's life. The loft can then be moved to new locations, and the bird can be taken hundreds of miles away from it. Despite the pigeon's and its loft's new locations, it will always return home. Scientists have many theories about how the bird employs this homing ability, including using the sun like a compass, detecting the Earth's

State-side army pigeon breeding lofts at Fort George Meade, a camouflage test on the left. *Courtesy Hayes Collection, Holt-Atherton Special Collections, University of the Pacific Library.*

magnetic field, or even using a type of olfactory navigation, but none of the theories have yet been scientifically proven. Training, however, is vital to the pigeon's abilities.

First, young homing pigeons are purchased or hatched in a loft, which becomes their permanent home, a place where they will always return. They are weaned in this loft and gradually allowed to fly short distances around the loft before returning to eat, a training mechanism somewhat similar to that for Pavlov's dogs. The young birds are fed only on their return to their loft, and are penalized by not being fed immediately if they do not enter the loft at once upon returning. Sometimes a particular call is used, a whistle blown, or a can of corn rattled to provide even more incentive for the bird to enter the loft immediately. This is also the time when, through much attention and handling, the birds begin to accustom themselves to the bird handlers. The military's goal with this type of training was to give the bird an incentive to bring the message back to its loft as soon as possible so that in the

field the Signal Corps could act on the communication immediately. The pigeons are trained at different distances, usually following a path the birds have to return by when coming back to their lofts. Birds are taken to different distances and dropped off, or "tossed," to fly home starting with half a mile, then one mile, then two, three, five, ten, sixteen, thirty-five, and increasing exponentially often up to 250 miles.

Homing pigeons do have limitations. They are unreliable in fog or bad weather, nor are they effective when flying at night. In fact, it was established during World War II that most pigeons would not travel at night, but rather stop at dusk and begin again at daybreak. Likewise, pigeons traveling at night over a body of water will usually alight on a ship at sea and start out again at dawn. Trainers tried to solve this dilemma by keeping pigeons in darkened lofts by day and illuminating the lofts at night, but most of these attempts were not successful. Another limitation is that most pigeons can only carry a message in one direction, i.e., back to their home loft. For

PIGEON FLIGHT RECORD

2nd Sheet

Band No. FtM-467   Color B ch   Sex C   Hatched 3/21/39

USA-39-

DATE OF FLIGHT -1939-	NATURE OF FLIGHT	COMPETITION		DISTANCE	POSITION AND SPEED	SPEED OF WINNING BIRD	TOTAL DISTANCE, ALL FLIGHTS
		Lofts	Birds				
8/12	GT-Train	2	54	37.3 SW	-	1137	234.8 272.1
8/13	GT-Train	2	52	45.3 S	late	967	317.4
8/15	DT-Train	1	34	56.0 W	12-1132	1276	373.4
8/17	ST-Train	3	76	63.5 SW	5-1282	1297	436.9
8/20	Race	22	226	90.1 SW	11th to loft-1219	1373	527.0
8/23	GT-Train	1	34	56.0 S	1-1381	Group-1345	583.0
8/27	Race	21	230	90.1 SW	3-961	966	673.1
8/29	Sig Com	1	16	15.0 NE	1200	-	688.1
8/31	ST-Train	2	53	45.3 SW	1-1331	-	733.4
9/3	Race	24	247	186.4 SW	7-1146	1190	919.8
9/5	GT-Train	2	49	28.5 W	-	1242	948.3
9/7	DT-Train	1	30	56.0 SW	3-1231	1239	1004.3
9/10	Race	24	220	186.4 SW	1-1228	-	1190.7

Example of a pigeon flight record taken from the technical manual *The Homing Pigeon,* TM 11-410, showing training flights and distances. *The National WWII Museum, 2008.273.*

intense, long-distance trips, the birds must have already had a long-time residence and completed enough training to be able to return to their loft as quickly as possible.

MILITARY TRAINING FOR HOMING PIGEONS

The military built or procured small lofts for incoming pigeons. These lofts had to be mobile and were therefore often constructed on top of military trailers, which could be attached to the company's jeeps and moved easily. The lofts were built to allow the birds to enter, but not leave, without the handler's participation. Signal pigeon companies were usually organized into seven-man sections with two jeeps, and therefore two combat-mobile lofts. Young birds, usually five weeks old, were settled into the lofts. When old enough to fly and accustomed to their handlers, they began learning to "trap" easily, "trapping" being the act of the pigeons returning to and immediately entering the loft. As soon as the birds entered the loft, they were given food as a reward for successfully returning during the training exercise. The birds, when very young, trap to the sound of the food, such as a can of corn being

Fifth Army combat mobile loft near olive trees and front line in Italy. *Courtesy Hayes Collection, Holt-Atherton Special Collections, University of the Pacific Library.*

U.S. Army Signal Corps pigeons inside a military loft. *National Archives photo.*

Mobile combat pigeon loft built on top of an army trailer, to be pulled by an army jeep. *National Archives photo.*

shaken. Later, they associate their loft with food, water, and protection, and therefore have a strong desire to return home to it.

Once the young birds trapped easily, their home lofts were moved short distances so that the birds did not become accustomed to their loft remaining in one place. When stronger and older, the birds were packed into carrying containers and taken a distance away to be released, as described earlier. The lofts were then moved greater distances away, up to twenty miles, while the birds were packed into carrying containers and released to return to the loft. Each time the birds were released on an expected line of advance, a preparatory path for their expected return from the front lines. At first, many birds were released together to help one another return home, but in the later stages of training, the birds were often released in just a pair. This was also the stage at

which handlers attached the message containers to the birds' legs so that they grew accustomed to flying while wearing them. All of this advanced military training was designed to *prevent* the bird's association with its home loft in one specific location. This way the birds could travel with advancing forces or aircraft, stay with them for multiple days if necessary, and, when released, still return to their home loft, despite the loft's probable move during the pigeon's time away.

The birds' military training occurred only in clear weather and during daylight hours. These conditions allowed the birds to familiarize themselves with the topography they were repeatedly flying over. Homing pigeons certainly utilize visual aids during their flight, and training helps them to emphasize this facility. With increasingly longer flights, pigeons develop an even stronger association of their lofts with home and therefore

Sign for the pigeon training center at Fort Monmouth, New Jersey. *Gift of John McIntire, 2011.209.004.*

PROCEDURE SIGNALS

The Signal Corps School
Fort Monmouth, N. J.

1936

RULES GOVERNING USE OF PROCEDURE SIGNALS

1. Procedure signals having an affirmative meaning are given a negative meaning by preceding the signal with ZZB.
EXAMPLE: ZZB ZGB XY means "Am not in communication with XY".

2. Procedure signals having an affirmative meaning can be given an interrogatory meaning by prefixing INT to the signal. Care must be taken that the signal thus constructed does not admit of wrong interpretation by the receiving station.
EXAMPLE: INT ZOF can be interpreted to mean "Shall I cease using speed key"?

3. Where the use of a procedure signal involves, or may involve, an additional transmission to complete or change the meaning of the signal, as indicated by blank space(s):

   a. All blank spaces not enclosed in parentheses require a transmission to fill them.

Procedure Signals booklet used at the Signal Corps school at Fort Monmouth. *Gift of John McIntire, 2011.209.005.*

ARMY SERVICE FORCES
Signal Corps—Army Pigeon Service Agency
WAR PIGEONS
Certificate of Service

This is to Certify that Homing Pigeon bearing leg band___ 63702 U*S 45 SC ___
has served with the Armed Forces of the United States of America during
WORLD WAR II

For the Chief Signal Officer: *Otto Meyer*

OTTO MEYER
Major, Signal Corps,
Commanding Officer,
Army Pigeon Service Agency.

Date___ MAY 10 1946 ___

Certificate of Service awarded to U.S. Signal Corps pigeon upon completion of military duties. *Courtesy Hayes Collection, Holt-Atherton Special Collections, University of the Pacific Library.*

return the messages faster. The bird returns to the loft, according to an April 1945 article published in *The Auk,* because it associates the loft with "food, water, a place to bathe, salt and grit which it is inordinately fond of, a place to roost (and each bird in the loft chooses its own particular place) and finally protection."

FORT MONMOUTH

Although birds were trained every day in the field, the beginning of their military service occurred at Fort Monmouth, New Jersey. This was the army's main pigeon hangar for the Signal Corps Pigeon Service. The Signal Corps expanded its roles in communication by recruiting specialists from the telephone industry, cameramen from the movie industry, and pigeon handlers from pigeon fanciers' associations throughout the United States. Pigeoneers—persons who care for and manage pigeons, especially those in military service—were in charge of the breeding, training, housing, and care of the homing pigeons. According to the World War II army manual on homing pigeons, a pigeoneer "must be kind, able to obtain

the confidence of the pigeons, patient, neat and firm." From Gen. John Pershing's call to action, the Signal Corps maintained a pigeon service beginning in 1917, centered at the U.S. Army Pigeon Breeding and Training Center at Fort Monmouth. The U.S. Army continued using pigeons as message carriers until 1957.

In the fall of 1936, Col. Clifford A. Poutre, chief pigeoneer of the U.S. Army Signal Corps Pigeon Service, was working under the tutelage of civilian pigeoneer Thomas Ross, a Scottish pigeon expert known throughout the world. After Ross's death, Poutre served as head of the Pigeon Breeding and Training Center from 1936 to 1943. By August 1941, Maj. John Shawvan of the Signal Corps, formerly a civilian pigeoneer, was also a high-ranking officer at the Pigeon Breeding and Training Center. Shawvan had organized the pigeon service of the French army at the end of World War I. That army prepared pigeons within simulated combat situations by training them like regular racing pigeons, but through smoke and shellfire. Three types of military pigeons were trained under these men: day-racing pigeons, night pigeons, and two-way pigeons. Major Shaw-

A Fifth Army soldier removes birds from an eight-bird airborne pigeon carrier. *Courtesy Hayes Collection, Holt-Atherton Special Collections, University of the Pacific Library.*

van claimed he developed the two-way training method in response to Hitler's Blitzkreig. Shaw-van explained that one of the chief goals of Blitzkreig warfare was the quick destruction of an enemy's communication lines, thus creating panic and confusion. The two-way pigeon can travel from the front line to deliver a message to headquarters, and then the same bird returns to the front line with the response. This type of training used a second basket of food and a later promise of food and reward at a specific location. Through these methods, the bird could fly back and forth between its home loft and the stationary basket, but this training was not particularly successful or useful with soldiers constantly on the move.

In conjunction with the pigeoneers' program of procuring, training, and supervising the pigeons, veterinary service for pigeons began at Fort Monmouth in 1941. This service was similar to the army's Quartermaster Corps remount service that supplied the army with horses, mules, and dogs. Veterinary service offered a solution to sick birds other than their immediate destruction, demonstrating the army's appreciation of these animals. Another large pigeon veterinary service was located in Camp Crowder, Missouri.

On January 9, 1942, the Signal Corps issued a call to civilian fanciers for healthy young pigeons to build up the army's pigeon service. The army offered five dollars for each bird, but remained hopeful that associations would instead donate the birds to aid their country in its new war. The call was quite successful; the fanciers' associations donated tens of thousands of birds, with individual shipments sometimes numbering in the thousands. An estimated 40,000 pigeons

Fifth Army soldier building combat mobile pigeon loft from plywood, on top of army trailer. *Courtesy Hayes Collection, Holt-Atherton Special Collections, University of the Pacific Library.*

were received from American pigeon breeders, which led to the creation of the Army Pigeon Service Agency, tasked with organizing the donations of birds. In February 1943, the Atlantic City Tuna Club, widely known at the time because of its ship-to-shore message service, donated all its carrier pigeons to the Signal Corps for military service. The Tuna Club was famous for carrying messages from fishing boats and yachts at sea back to the shore, with messages ranging from domestic notes to distress signals.

IN THE FIELD AND IN COMBAT

World War II saw extensive use of pigeons in combat. The Signal Corps issued combat lofts that could be quickly positioned to serve the army in any combat zone. Because these combat lofts were so important to training pigeons, and because U.S. Army trailers and materiel used in the construction of combat lofts was so desperately needed, in some theaters trailers were stolen from other military units at night and repainted as property of the Signal Corps. The loft was then

constructed using scrap material. In challenging locations such as the wet climate of the Central Pacific, these lofts often had to be remodeled to allow for air flow and sunlight. Loft sanitation was very important to the health of the birds.

The army's pigeoneers provided the front-line soldiers with birds as they prepared to enter combat. The soldiers would march or fly into battle with one or multiple pigeons, either in a single carrying pouch or in boxes designed for specific deployments. It might seem odd to jump out of a plane with a pigeon bound to your chest, but the pigeons' homing abilities were so strong that, if not restrained, they would immediately fly home and thus be of no use to the soldiers. If a soldier or airman needed to send a message by pigeon, he would simply write his message and attach it to the bird, which, once released, would return to its home loft. The pigeoneers would await their birds and immediately relay the communication to Signal Corps headquarters.

The Army Veterinary Service paid close attention to the pigeons' health while overseas. All feed, a factor deemed essential to the birds'

U.S. pigeoneer introducing "squeakers" to their new combat pigeon loft in Italy. *Courtesy Hayes Collection, Holt-Atherton Special Collections, University of the Pacific Library.*

performance, had to be harvested, checked, and shipped from the United States to prevent any bird diseases from wiping out the army's pigeons. Unfortunately, the feed, often sent in burlap sacks, easily became moldy or infested with bugs or rodents. To make up for the imbalance of nutrients because of pests, 45,000 multivitamin capsules were issued to each pigeon company near the end of the war.

Signal pigeon companies were usually split up into sections with jeeps and mobile combat lofts, then subdivided into three combat platoons per section. These birds were trained at least once every day, even near the front lines. Pigeon companies in combat traveled with the infantry to the front lines. Breeding was an important factor in pigeons returning to their permanent

lofts; therefore, these lofts had to be accounted for in the field, too. Troops often ran out of bird housing and used any kind of building that would work as a breeding loft, as the front was moving too fast to stay anywhere long. In the breeding lofts the birds would produce "squabs," baby birds that were tagged with an aluminum identification band. Each breeding loft contained one hundred pairs of birds, and one pigeoneer was assigned to two breeding lofts. When the squabs developed and could eat on their own, they were deemed "squeakers" and moved to the mobile combat lofts, which served as their home for the remainder of their lives.

Combat pigeons had very short life spans as they were preyed upon by both natural and unnatural enemies. They were constantly threat-

War correspondent sending war coverage via pigeon. *Courtesy Hayes Collection, Holt-Atherton Special Collections, University of the Pacific Library.*

Shown here in the hold of a ship are 1,500 pigeons of a signal pigeon company arriving in New Caledonia in 1942, new members of the Americal Division. *National Archives photo.*

ened by artillery fire, anti-aircraft fire, and direct hits by Axis riflemen as they flew over enemy territory. They were also hunted by their natural predator, the hawk, either those in the wild or the Axis's trained birds. In addition, the Germans were training falcons to intercept pigeons delivering messages. When these predator birds discovered the field locations of the breeding and combat lofts, U.S. soldiers shot at them with shotguns, not only to kill the hawks and falcons, but also to accustom the pigeons to the sound of gunfire for their future combat duties.

The American army supplied pigeons not only for its own soldiers, but also for the British and French armies. Throughout the war there was high demand for pigeons from the mountainous terrains of North Africa to the Mediterranean to the jungles of the China-Burma-India theater and the Central Pacific, as well as from Europe. The Signal Corps used pigeons to maintain communication when all other means failed in these foreign and difficult terrains. In Normandy, the British dropped many American pigeons from planes in specially designed parachutes to be picked up by members of the French resistance. Once found, given a message, and released by the Resistance, they were on their way back to England with important information on German strengths and weaknesses. Pigeons were also faithfully used by war correspondents to send stories back from the front lines as fast as possible.

Impressive numbers of pigeons were used during World War II. The Central Pacific region's numbers are a good example. In July 1942, the 279th Signal Pigeon Company arrived in the Central Pacific with 1,920 birds sent from a breeding center in Hawaii. By December of that year there were 2,278 pigeons in the Pacific theater, and in December 1943, 3,426 pigeons. In December 1944, approximately 2,300 surplus pigeons were shipped to the Southwest Pacific area as well.

FAMOUS PIGEONS

War pigeons often flew through harm's way to return home, no matter the cost. Many pigeons were mortally wounded as they carried important messages around the globe. Here are the stories of three American pigeons that were shot at, caught in crossfire, and hunted down by German falcons. They lost eyes, feet, and other body parts, but continued their missions nonetheless.

LADY ASTOR

Taken to the front lines with a combat unit in North Africa, Lady Astor was released with an urgent message. She completed a flight of sixty miles even after being shot by pellets, breaking her leg, and losing half the feathers from one wing. Once home, she alighted onto the roof of the loft and immediately collapsed, having delivered her message safely. She was later nursed back to health and retired from active service.

YANK

When American soldiers stormed and retook Gafsa, Tunisia, Yank was released with the message of victory. He flew back to headquarters at Tebessa, Algeria, ninety-eight miles away, to deliver the news ahead of all other means of communication.

G.I. JOE

Savior of a brigade of the British 56th Infantry Division, G.I. Joe was probably the most famous American pigeon of the war. G.I. Joe carried an urgent message to the Allied air-support command center after radio contact was lost. The Italian city of Colvi was occupied by British troops on October 18, 1943, at 10 a.m., well ahead of schedule. The U.S. Air Force was scheduled to bomb

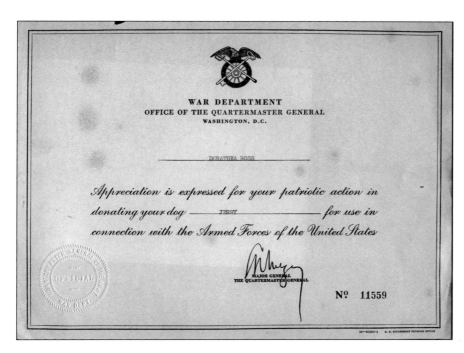

Certificate of appreciation given to Dorathea Ross by the War Department, Office of the Quartermaster General, for donating her dog Jerry for use by the U.S. military. *The National WWII Museum, 2009.567.*

Dogs were trained with different collars; through repetition they learned what each collar signified. This flat leather collar meant that it was time to go to work—there would be no playing and no barking. *The National WWII Museum, 2008.447.*

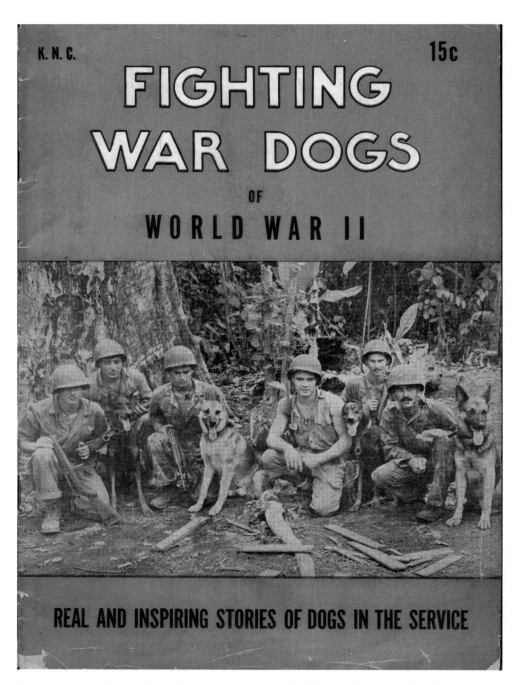

The interest in war dogs and their efforts was keen in the 1940s. This small booklet published in 1944 by the U.S. Sales Company tells the stories of several war-dog heroes and gives some insight into the training of the dogs and the conditions in which they were fighting. *The National WWII Museum, 2008.396.*

As early as 1944, people were eager to express their appreciation for the work of U.S. military war dogs. In that year Clayton G. Going wrote *Dogs at War,* an "authoritative book on the amazing exploits of man's best friend in this war." *The National WWII Museum, 2008.275.*

WAR DOG FUND

DOGS FOR DEFENSE, Inc.

"BOOGIE"

Having contributed $ 1.00 for the procurement of Dogs for the Armed Forces of the United States of America, is awarded this certificate as a SEAMAN (NAVY) of the War Dog Fund.

Nº 24785   DOGS FOR DEFENSE, Inc.

© GOES 200

WAR DOG FUND

DOGS FOR DEFENSE, Inc.

"STINKY"

Having contributed $ 2.00 for the procurement of Dogs for the Armed Forces of the United States of America, is awarded this certificate as a PRIVATE FIRST of the CLASS (WOMEN'S DIVISION War Dog Fund. MARINES)

Nº 24786   DOGS FOR DEFENSE, Inc.

© GOES 200

Dogs for Defense war-dog fund certificates. *Gift of Nora Brennecke, 2011.247.004.*

Front and back of a Dogs for Defense tag for a dog collar. Two of these tags were given to Wendell Brennecke for his contribution to the war-dog fund, to be worn by his dogs Boogie and Stinky. *Gift of Nora Brennecke, 2011.247.004.*

James M. Austin, *Chairman*
WAR DOG FUND

Telephone:
PLaza 8-2292

WAR DOG FUND

DOGS FOR DEFENSE, INC.

250 PARK AVENUE
(ROOM 511)
NEW YORK 17, N. Y.

Could your dog - as a
member of the War Dog
Fund - enroll 3 more
members among your
friends' dogs? For en-
rolling 3 new members,
your dog will be award-
ed the new War Dog
Fund STAR OF MERIT
Certificate.
Sign your name and
address and your dog's
certificate number on
enlistment blank to get
credit for enlistments.

Mr. Wendell S. Brennecke,
Walhalla,
South Carolina

March 20, 1944

Dear Mr. Brennecke:

We have received your contribution of $_____3.00_____
"BOOGIE"
"STINKY"_____ is now a
SEAMAN (NAVY)
PRIVATE FIRST CLASS (WOMEN'S DIVISION in the War Dog Fund.
                    MARINE CORPS)
                       24785
Enclosed find certificate #_____24786_____ and a tag
for your dog's collar.

We wish to express our appreciation for your generous
co-operation in this worthy cause. If you would care
to promote your dog at any future time, kindly send us
his certificate number and the additional money to
cover rank selected, and we will credit you with your
original contribution.

Please be sure to have your friends and neighbors enlist
their dogs in our WAR DOG FUND. (Blanks enclosed)

Mrs. J. D. Verner
Walhalla, S.C.

Yours very truly,

James M. Austin

James M. Austin, Chairman

JMA/vm

Thank-you letter from Dogs for Defense to Wendell Brennecke for his contribution of $3.00 in the names of his dogs Boogie and Stinky. *Gift of Nora Brennecke, 2011.247.004.*

U.S. Marine Corps war-dog platoon patch. *Gift of Col. Keith M. Schmedemann, 2009.384.*

TM 10–396

WAR DEPARTMENT

TECHNICAL MANUAL

WAR DOGS

1 July 1943

War Dogs, Technical Manual 10-396, outlines the mission of war-dog training as well as basic training principles, specialized training principles, and how to use them. *The National WWII Museum, 2006.256.*

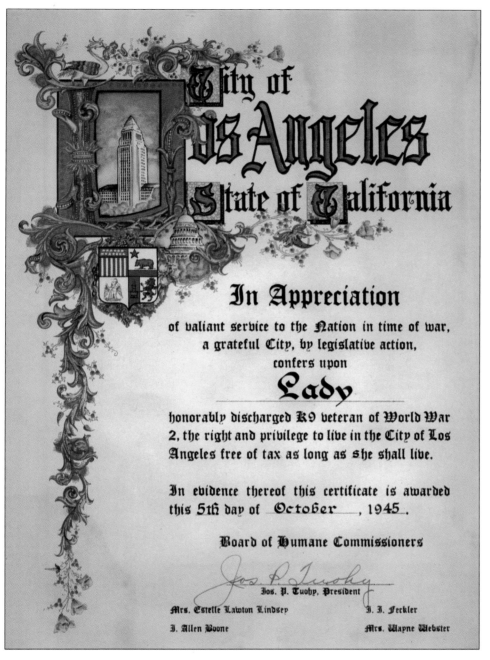

City of Los Angeles
State of California

In Appreciation

of valiant service to the Nation in time of war,
a grateful City, by legislative action,
confers upon

Lady

honorably discharged K9 veteran of World War
2, the right and privilege to live in the City of Los
Angeles free of tax as long as she shall live.

In evidence thereof this certificate is awarded
this 5th day of October , 1945 .

Board of Humane Commissioners

Jos. P. Tuohy
Jos. P. Tuohy, President

Mrs. Estelle Lawton Lindsey   J. J. Feckler

J. Allen Boone   Mrs. Wayne Webster

Certificate of appreciation for Lady from Los Angeles, California, for her service as a war dog. *The National WWII Museum, 2008.285.*

Veterinarian bag and roll of surgical instruments used by Lt. William Putney. Although not the official platoon veterinarian, Putney used his knowledge of veterinary medicine to treat dogs under his command. *Gift of Betsy Putney, 2010.215.*

Hiram Boone's personal camera, an Agfa Ansco Shur-Shot D6 with custom leather case, carried by Boone throughout his travels in Burma and China with the Mars Task Force. The camera and case were mailed to him overseas by his parents. He carried it slung on the pommel of his mule's saddle. All of the images in this book credited to Boone were taken with this camera. *Gift of Hiram Vance Boone, 2002.210.034.*

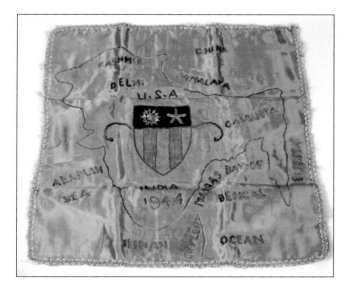

An embroidered pillow cover, a souvenir of Hiram Boone's arrival in India, depicting a map of India and surrounding countries along with a China-Burma-India military patch in the center. *Gift of Hiram Vance Boone, 2002.210.035.*

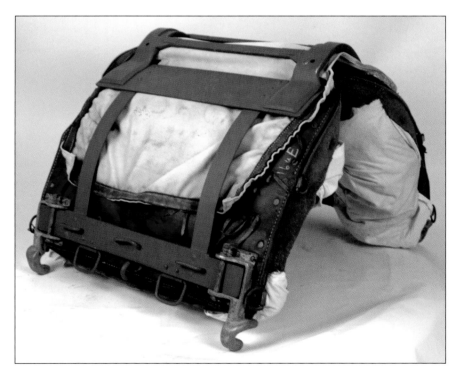

The army cargo pack saddle, with all its accouterments, weighs nearly 100 pounds. Mules usually carried a payload of about 200 more pounds; the muleskinner made sure the weight carried was less than one-third the animal's weight. At times this load was measured at up to 350 pounds. Stronger mules were used for carrying the artillery—the heaviest and most awkward load. *The National WWII Museum, 2007.330.001.*

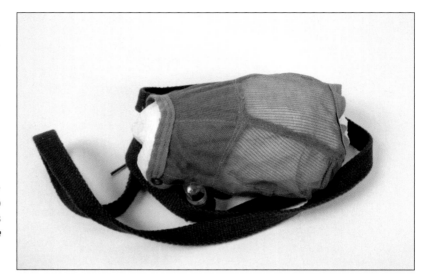

This pigeon vest was used by para-troopers and Signal Corps men to transport one pigeon; it also has a message capsule attached. *The National WWII Museum, 2006.121.*

Signal Corps book used to write messages placed in capsules and then carried by the pigeons. The messages were carbon-copied in triplicate and included dates, times, and signatures. *Gift of Eric Bechler, 2000.060.*

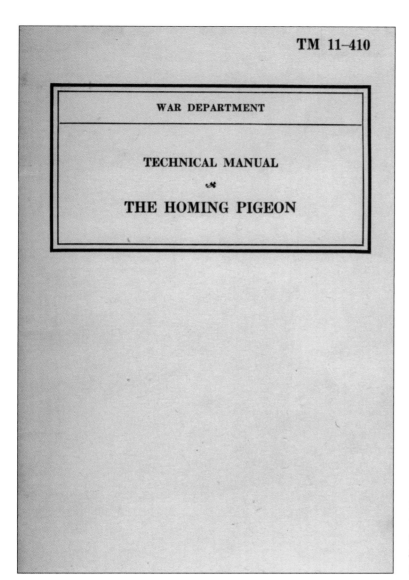

TM 11–410

WAR DEPARTMENT

TECHNICAL MANUAL

THE HOMING PIGEON

The Homing Pigeon, Technical Manual 11-410, outlines the purpose of homing pigeons as well as their care, training, and breeding. *The National WWII Museum, 2008.273.*

Message capsules were attached to a pigeon's leg for safekeeping during the flight. *Gift of Walter F. Zagol, 0000.015, and Mignon Lamar, 2000.082.*

Cardboard pigeon carrier used for carrying two pigeons. Shipped flat to conserve space, the container has instructions for assembly and for sending messages printed on the exterior. *The National WWII Museum, 2006.121.*

Wooden two-bird pigeon carrier with hinged lid and floor— a more lasting version of the cardboard carrier. The bars at the front of the container slide up and down for access and support the food and water tray. *The National WWII Museum, 2008.319.*

An airborne pigeon carrier designed for dropping the pigeons down to earth by a small parachute. The carrier held eight birds; the galvanized metal mesh allowed air to flow through the container. *The National WWII Museum, 2008.418.*

Pin in support of Gen. Jonathan M. Wainwright. *Gift of Patricia De Groot, 2007.291.*

Horse wearing gas mask, as pictured in *Doughboy to GI,* by Kenneth Lewis.

Gas mask designed specifically for horses. The threat of chemical warfare was high during World War II, and the U.S. military wanted to protect its animals as well as its soldiers. *The National WWII Museum, 2008.446.*

Eisenhower-style jacket worn by Dr. Joseph H. Groveman, with his Veterinary Corps lapel insignia and SHAEF shoulder patch. Groveman enlisted in the army in 1940. Upon his graduation from veterinary school in April 1943, he immediately reported for active duty. His first assignment was as a meat and dairy inspector, but soon he was sent to Bavaria. While there, he helped with the denazification of the German meat and dairy industry and the German veterinary service. *Gift of Dr. Joseph H. Groveman, 2007.318.*

Insignia of the U.S. Army Veterinary Corps. *Gift of Dr. Joseph H. Groveman, 2007.318.*

Groveman at work in Germany. *Gift of Dr. Joseph H. Groveman, 2007.318.*

Originally designed by George McClellan for the U.S. Army in the 1850s, the McClellan saddle continued to be a standard army saddle through World War II. The hole in the middle allowed for more efficient and easier fitting of the saddle to the horse and greater comfort for the rider. *The National WWII Museum, 2008.444.*

The famous Yank on the left, and Lady Astor on the right. *Courtesy Hayes Collection, Holt-Atherton Special Collections, University of the Pacific Library.*

the city an hour later to aid the British attack. Attempts by radio to cancel the bombing failed. G.I. Joe, borrowed from the Americans who accompanied the British troops, was released with the important message to cancel the bombing. The bird flew a mile a minute for twenty miles and arrived just in time to alert the 15th Air Force to reroute the bombers, saving the lives of nearly one thousand British soldiers from an Allied bombing. For his bravery, G.I. Joe was awarded the Dickin Medal of Gallantry by the Lord Mayor of London. G.I. Joe was the only American animal to receive the Dickin Medal. He died in 1961, at age eighteen, and can be seen today, mounted, in the Historical Center at Fort Monmouth, New Jersey.

The following four American birds were cited as outstanding examples of courageous feathered flyers in a 1946 War Department release.

BURMA QUEEN

Burma Queen saved the lives of hundreds of U.S. troops under attack near the border of Thailand and Burma. Amid heavy fighting, Burma Queen was dropped from a B-25 Mitchell bomber to Allied forces who had destroyed their radios and codes to prevent their capture by the Japanese. The rear Allied command post had sent out the bomber to search for the group. The search was successful, and the pigeon was parachuted down to aid the soldiers. Burma Queen flew over 320 miles through Burmese mountains to bring the troops' urgent message for help and news of their situation back to Allied headquarters. She was released at 6 a.m. and made it back to her loft at 3 p.m. She flew many other important dispatches during some of the worst fighting in that theater.

CAPTAIN LEDERMAN

Captain Lederman was hatched in Burma in 1944 and flew as far as 320 miles in a day carrying vital information about enemy troop movements, heavy-gun placement, and supplies in the mountainous terrain of Burma. He, like many other pigeons, was dropped via parachute or bamboo container to patrols operating behind enemy lines gathering information. The information would be attached to his leg, and this little bird would fly over the rugged mountains and deep jungles to give Allied command the intelligence on a timely basis.

JUNGLE JOE

Jungle Joe began his flying career at four months. The airborne patrol he was with lost its radio operator deep behind enemy lines in the jungles of Burma. Jungle Joe thus became their only contact with headquarters. The patrol collected vital information for a week, all while keeping the bird confined in its 4" x 4" x 14" jump container so as not to lose him. On the seventh day, they sent all the intelligence with Jungle Joe to headquarters, with the result that Allied troops captured a large section of Burma. Joe had flown 225 miles, over some of the highest mountains in the country, to give Allied commanders the intelligence they needed. Joe's news also included the location of the soldiers, so another radio operator was parachuted in and the group was once again in direct contact with headquarters.

BLACKIE HALLIGAN

Blackie Halligan was hatched at Fort Monmouth, New Jersey, and was later shipped via the West Coast through the Fiji Islands and New Caledonia to Guadalcanal with the 132nd Infantry Regiment, 33rd Infantry Division. Blackie flew many short missions, carrying all types of messages. One day, despite being severely wounded, he carried a vital message about the location of three hundred Japanese troops. The journey to headquarters should have taken just twenty minutes, but Blackie was shot down by Japanese fire. Five hours later, the maimed and bloody bird managed to complete its trip bearing the important message. Gen. Alexander Patch, commander of the Americal Division, visited Blackie's coop and decorated him for bravery under fire. Blackie returned to the United States after the war by special courier on orders of General Patch.

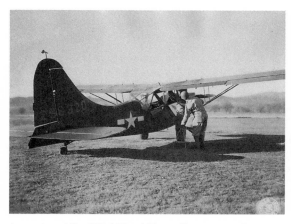

A member of the 283rd Signal Pigeon Company carries cages of pigeons to a plane from which they will be dropped during training maneuvers at Hunter Liggett Military Reservation in California. *Gift in memory of Maurice T. White, Captain, U.S. Army Signal Corps, 2011.065.1858.*

A nine-foot parachute carrying a cage of six pigeons descends to troops training in difficult mountainous terrain in California. *Gift in memory of Maurice T. White, Captain, U.S. Army Signal Corps, 2011.065.1859.*

Two pigeon cages supported by a parachute are retrieved after being dropped from a plane during training maneuvers. *Gift in memory of Maurice T. White, Captain, U.S. Army Signal Corps, 2011.065.1820.*

A Signal Corps pigeon is removed from a cage with five other pigeons after a successful drop by parachute. *Gift in memory of Maurice T. White, Captain, U.S. Army Signal Corps, 2011.065.1855.*

Cavalry troops on horseback, Fort Benning, Georgia, 1935. *Gift of John Pope, 2002.307.*

4. The Last Cavalry Charge

In 1895, Gen. William H. Carter stated in his book *The US Cavalry Horse,* "Men high in authority, dreaming of future wars, foresaw the troop horse and the army mule displaced by the bicycle and automobile . . . experience has not justified the views of the theorists." When General Carter wrote these words, there was still a great demand for horses and mules in the U.S. military, but ultimately, Carter was mistaken. As the American military progressed into the twentieth century, the nation's horse stock would be reduced from 25 million animals in 1920 to 14 million animals by 1940. This reduction was part of a national trend away from animal-powered transportation and labor to a mechanized system. The average American citizen as well as the U.S. military was moving toward motorization. Use of the horse in military operations continued to decline, and after the 1940 Louisiana Maneuvers, cavalry units were slowly reorganized into armored corps.

There was heated debate among top-ranking officials about the elimination of horses and cavalry units from the army altogether. The army did keep a few horse-equipped cavalry units. There were two divisions, two regiments, and two mixed horse-and-motor transportation regiments with a total of 16,800 horses. One horse-equipped unit, the 26th Cavalry Regiment, Philippine Scouts, would see significant action during World War II in the battle for the Philippines. This regiment would lead the last cavalry charge in the history of the U.S. Army in the village of Morong on January 16, 1942.

THE PHILIPPINES

In 1941, as the Japanese continued to wage war on China, their need for oil, rubber, and other natural resources became desperate. Both the United States and Great Britain had placed embargoes on these items and frozen Japanese assets, making it increasingly harder for them to acquire the raw materials they needed to continue their war efforts in China. The Japanese took bold steps to ensure their gains in China would not be lost by invading the island nations in the Pacific. They hoped to secure oil from Borneo, Java, and Sumatra, along with rubber from Burma and Malaya. To secure shipping lanes for these raw materials, Japan invaded the American-controlled Philippine Islands.

Gen. Jonathan M. Wainwright was com-

Unit photograph of the 26th Cavalry Regiment (Philippine Scouts), Fort Stotsenburg, Philippines, 1937. *Courtesy American Historical Collection, Rizal Library, Ateneo de Manila University.*

mander of the Philippine Division, assigned to the post in 1940. Nicknamed "Skinny," Wainwright was a 1906 graduate of West Point and a World War I veteran. His assignment as commander represented a significant achievement for Wainwright, with about 7,500 soldiers under his command. These soldiers were mostly Philippine Scouts, or native Filipinos who fought under the American flag. Also assigned to Wainwright was the 26th Cavalry Regiment, one of the last horse-mounted cavalries in the U.S. Army. Wainwright was a traditionalist when it came to the cavalry. His sentiments were that horse-mounted cavalry were some of the finest, most select, and most well-trained soldiers in the military. In his memoir, *General Wainwright's Story,* he says of this unit that they were "to fight as few cavalry units ever fought."

One officer of the 26th Cavalry Regiment was Lt. Edwin Price Ramsey. Like Wainwright, Ramsey believed the horse-mounted cavalry to be a superior unit of the military. He took great pride in the horsemanship skills he had learned at the Oklahoma Military Academy. Despite the move toward mechanized cavalry, Ramsey held fast to his passion for horses and the work they could do in a military environment. He stated in his memoir, *Lieutenant Ramsey's War,* "The cavalry was elite, the crown of the service. Its history was the schema of the nation. The cavalry had been born in the Revolution, opened the frontier, fused the Union, and conquered the West. America was

made on horseback, carved by mounted soldiers; our identity as a people was dictated from the saddle." It was with this passion to remain in a mounted unit that he volunteered to go to the Philippines in April 1941.

Ramsey was assigned to lead Troop G, 2nd Squadron, of the 26th Cavalry Regiment. His troop consisted of twenty-seven men, all Filipinos, whom Ramsey was to train in mounted and dismounted drill. The men were disciplined, some having served close to thirteen years in the 26th, and Ramsey enjoyed working with them. He wrote, "The 26th was the elite regiment; everyone knew it, and we all were anxious and proud to serve in it." It was with this troop that Ramsey was assigned his horse Bryn Awryn, a chestnut gelding fifteen and a half hands tall and with a small white blaze on his forehead. Bryn Awryn was powerful and well schooled, clever and aggressive, with the ability to turn on a dime.

Drill training sessions were long for both the soldiers and the horses. The men would load the horses onto trucks and drive long distances to various training areas. At first, the units trained with blank ammunition to get the horses accustomed to the noise of gunfire. Once the horses had been desensitized to the noise, the troops began using live rounds. They practiced various cavalry maneuvers including the iconic charge. American cavalries had not charged since the Pancho Villa Expedition in Mexico some twenty years earlier. The 26th practiced the maneuver

Lt. Edwin Price Ramsey. *Courtesy Lt. Edwin Price Ramsey.*

hundred casualties from the raid. The Japanese began landing on December 10, 1941, on the northern part of the island of Luzon.

THE WAR PLAN

The military was somewhat prepared for this situation. In the 1930s, authorities had drawn up various plans in case of conflict between Japan and the United States on Luzon. They used a form of color coding where each color represented a different situation. In the spring of 1941, War Plan Orange III (WPO-III) called for Americans not to fight except in central Luzon. WPO-III was to be implemented in a situation involving only the United States and Japan. The plan reflected the feelings of military leaders that the best defense of Luzon was on the Bataan Peninsula, which overlooked Manila Bay. The city of Corregidor, located on a small island just off the end of the peninsula, was the most strategic point. By October 1941, WPO-III was outdated and the Rainbow V plan was in place. This plan kept many tactical elements of WPO-III, including the measured retreat to Corregidor, but recognized the global scale of the impending situation.

The WPO-III and Rainbow V plans held that the army's priority was to protect the entrance to Manila Bay. Next, they should prevent Japanese troops from landing on Luzon. If they were unable to do so, they should begin various delaying maneuvers to allow as many troops as possible to safely withdraw to the Bataan Peninsula. As they went, they were to hold back the Japanese from entering Bataan. The plan also accounted for the moving of ample supplies to Corregidor to keep the troops provisioned for six months.

The traditional role of the cavalry is to delay the enemy and defend territory. The 26th Cavalry would be central to the war plan. The regiment would also be used to provide reconnaissance

despite its lack of use, knowing that it was the "ultimate weapon" of the cavalry. Ramsey stated, "We worked at it until we could unleash it on an instant at full fury."

On December 7, 1941, in the Philippine capital city of Manila, Ramsey and Bryn Awryn and the Troop G team played a friendly game of polo against the local Manila Polo Club. General Wainwright was on hand to keep score. As the day dawned on December 8, they received word of the bombing of Pearl Harbor, where the local time was 6 a.m., December 7. Just hours after the attack on Pearl Harbor, the Japanese began various air assaults on the Philippines. One particular attack at Clark Air Field, located just north of Manila, raged for two hours. It destroyed almost the entire airfield and hit a store of about two hundred U.S. Navy torpedoes that were needed to repel the Japanese navy. There were some five

and security, and to raid, attack, and pursue the enemy. However, the mounted cavalry were at a disadvantage considering the terrain of the central Luzon, where much of the battle would take place. The open, muddy plains of the island's center were much more suited to tanks and artillery, but significant numbers of these were not available to Wainwright at the time. Ramsey stated, "It was a lesson that had been carved from the flesh of men and mounts in France in World War I. Yet, in the Philippines, cavalry remained elite, held in place by tradition and untested by modern war."

TROOP G IN ACTION

As Clark Air Field was being bombed, Troop G was moving out of Fort Stotsenburg to the village of Bongabon about 120 miles northeast. Troop G was to relieve Troop B, which was headed back to Fort Stotsenburg. As Ramsey's troop reached Bongabon, he was given orders to defend Baler Bay about fifty miles farther northeast. He was to take command of the local police, organize a defense, and repel any Japanese invasion as long as possible. He had with him twenty-seven mounted Filipinos, two machine guns, and a staff car with a radio. By the time the troop reached Baler Bay fifteen hours later, both men and horses were hungry, anxious, and out of sorts.

Ramsey set up a command post and quickly got defenses organized. Within a week, on December 17, Japanese Zeros began strafing the area. Ramsey ordered the horses moved farther back into the woods as bullets ripped through the village on the bay. The Zeros circled, flying higher, and then began dropping bombs. Ramsey describes the scene in his memoir: "The whole bay convulsed with fire and explosion and thick clouds of smoke." The attack lasted fifteen to twenty minutes, taking the lives of many villagers. Amazingly, none of the Philippine Scouts or

their horses had been hit. Ramsey ordered his men to stay on high alert.

Just over two weeks later, Ramsey and his mounted troops were ordered to withdraw to Bongabon, as the Japanese had come ashore on the western side of the island at Lingayen Gulf. The majority of the 26th had been battling the Japanese for days on the western side, taking heavy losses.

Troop B along with most of the rest of the 26th fought hard to stave off more Japanese landings in Lingayen Gulf. They worked with a small tank force to hold the city of Damortis; however, anti-tank fire allowed the Japanese to take control of the city. Now the Japanese were advancing from two directions on the town of Rosario—along the coastal road from Damortis and inland from forces moving south. The Philippine Scouts continued to perform delaying maneuvers that allowed their troops to move out of the area. In *The Fall of the Philippines*, Louis Morton states, "All the honors in the first day's fight had gone to the Japanese. Only the Scouts of the 26th Cavalry had offered any serious opposition to the successful completion of the Japanese plan."

In the Philippines, Japanese air assaults had decimated the air force component of the U.S. Armed Forces in the Far East (USAFFE), and therefore little could be done to stop or even hinder the invading Japanese forces. Reinforcements from the USAFFE struggled to get to the Philippine Division and the 26th Cavalry Regiment. During the delay, the Filipino line broke and troops fled to the rear, abandoning their guns. Troops were pushed twenty miles south to Binalonan. Here, however, the 26th Cavalry was able to stop the advancing Japanese troops despite their lack of anti-tank weapons. The regiment routed the Japanese infantry and inflicted heavy casualties. Even with more tanks and troops, the Japanese were unable to advance.

Southeast Luzon, Philippines.
Map by Mary Lee Eggart.

When USAFFE reinforcements arrived, the 26th was so deeply entrenched in the battle the troops were unable to fall back and allow fresh forces to take over. They waged war for hours and saw their number cut almost in half, from 842 to just 450. Despite these heavy losses, they continued to fight in various delaying actions so that supply trains and the wounded could be evacuated from Binalonan. By nightfall, their battle was over. The Japanese began to enter the town. The regiment had lost more than a quarter of its officers and men and over half of its horses. Troop B, which Ramsey had relieved only three weeks before, nearly ceased to exist.

It was time to retreat to Corregidor in accord with the WPO-III plan. Part of the plan was an orderly withdrawal to the Bataan Peninsula. The plan laid out five defensive lines that were to be held by the troops. As troops and supplies came through the lines, the army was to fall back to the next line, destroying roads and bridges as they went. In particular, Wainwright had to ensure that troops in the south had time to cross the central plain and reach the peninsula. If the troops did not make it, or Wainwright fell back too soon, he would cut off half of the troops on Luzon. Each line was strategically placed to take advantage of the island's topography. All lines fell

Lt. Edwin Price Ramsey and his horse, Bryn Awryn, 1941. *Courtesy Lt. Edwin Price Ramsey.*

on high ground and were about a day's march apart. The plan called for Wainwright to hold a line only long enough for the Japanese to prepare for an attack. Just as they were ready, Wainwright was to move, thus subverting the attack. The aim was merely to delay the Japanese rather than try to defeat them.

As Wainwright was on the western side of Luzon steadily falling back to the Bataan Peninsula, Ramsey was on the eastern side of the island, trying to ensure that his Troop G made it over to Bataan before the Japanese troops pinched him off from the peninsula.

As December marched on, so did the Japanese, landing more soldiers on the island and mov-

ing troops farther south. When Ramsey reached Bongabon, he offloaded his horses and the troops began pushing toward Cabanatuan, where they were to meet up with other parts of the 26th Cavalry. Unfortunately, Cabanatuan had been hit the day before, and Ramsey and his troops found the city in ruins. Amid the destruction was more than a million pounds of provisions for the troops heading to Bataan. As Troop G marched on, they were spotted by Mitsubishi A6M Zeros, which strafed and bombed them. They reached the village of San Isidro some seventy-two hours later. Here Ramsey saw the remnants of the rest of the 26th, who had been fighting on the other side of the island. "It was a literal skeleton of the regiment I had joined six months before. The men were haggard and showed signs of malnutrition. The horses that were left could scarcely walk."

Ramsey and the remaining men and horses of the 26th remounted after only a few days' rest. By New Year's Day 1942, they were ordered into one of Wainwright's lines. There were only enough horses for three mounted troops; everyone else was transferred to a motorized unit. Ramsey still had Bryn Awryn and was named commander of Troop G. Their charge was to guard Porac, one of two key towns at the top of the Bataan Peninsula. Ramsey and the men of Troop G were to keep the Japanese on the western side of Luzon from entering Bataan. They fought hard for days on little sleep and scarce supplies of food and forage for the horses.

On January 4, 1942, a huge push by Japanese forces under the command of General Masaharu Homma crumpled the 21st Infantry Division. The loss of the 21st and their subsequent crossing of the Layac River put the 26th in a desperate rearguard fight. As soon as the regiment crossed the river, Wainwright ordered the bridge destroyed. It was vital to hold this new line at the Layac River so that more troops and supplies could make their way down the peninsula. Ramsey and the 26th continued to stay on the western side of the island. They had little natural cover and on January 7 found themselves in the midst of a pitched battle. The U.S. 23rd Field Artillery was behind them shelling the Japanese line, while the Japanese, in front of Ramsey, were returning fire. Shrapnel began to fall on the men and horses, shredding the horses' sides. The horses screeched and galloped away in fear. The barrage continued for eight hours with horses and men being hit. Two men were killed and several wounded; twenty-one horses were killed. Bryn Awryn survived. The 23rd Field Artillery had been annihilated, losing four of its five guns.

The next days of the 26th Cavalry were spent in a desperate scramble to rendezvous with the other infantry division in the area. They struggled through dense jungles and deep ravines. Often the men had to lead their horses as the trails were steep and difficult to negotiate. During this time the men went without eating. Ramsey wrote, "Every scrap of food we found we gave to our mounts, for to a cavalryman his horse is his survival." On January 9 they were able to connect with scout cars from their regiment. Upon meeting up with his regimental commanders, Ramsey learned that the cavalry's delay tactics had worked and Wainwright's line was in place. The remaining men of the 26th were to move on and continue to protect the western flank of the defense line.

Bataan was now filled with more than a hundred thousand troops and civilians escaping the Japanese. The four-hundred-square-mile peninsula was packed with people, but supplies were scarce. By mid-January it was estimated that there was only enough ammunition, food, and forage for the animals to last four months. At the end of January, that estimate dropped to just an eleven-day supply. There were constant reassurances that a convoy of ships was due to bring aid and supplies and also to get troops off the island. What many did not realize was that the bombing of the Pearl Harbor fleet meant there were no ships to come to their aid. One fatal flaw of the war plan was the heavy reliance on the ships of Pearl Harbor to rescue those in the Philippines.

On January 10, Ramsey and the 26th arrived in Bagac and received word that the Japanese had landed more troops farther north at Olongopo. They provisioned their horses and began searching the countryside of the western coast of Bataan. They were on half rations, exhausted and growing leaner. Ramsey states, "By January 15 the animals were scarcely able to lift their feet over

Gen. Jonathan M. Wainwright looks on as Gen. Douglas MacArthur signs the terms of the Japanese surrender in September 1945. Wainwright was forced to surrender to the Japanese in May 1942 and to march to a POW camp in northern Luzon in what was known as the Bataan Death March. Wainwright remained a Japanese prisoner-of-war until August 1945. *Gift of John Laborde, 2009.135.*

the vines that clogged the trails, and the troopers slumbered in their saddles." It was painful for Ramsey to watch the flanks of Bryn Awryn subside and his haunches droop.

Troop G returned to headquarters and was given a much-deserved rest. Ramsey, however, with his indispensable knowledge of the terrain, stayed on to lead the remnants of Troops E and F with twenty-seven weary Filipino cavalrymen. General Wainwright gave orders to reoccupy the village of Morong. Wainwright remembered

Ramsey's skill at polo from the match held in December and ordered him to take his unit to reconnoiter the village before troops moved in. The dry season had come to Bataan, and as Troop E moved out, the dust from the coastal road clogged the nostrils and coated the throats of the horses.

Ramsey's platoon was in the lead and reached the village first. It initially looked deserted, but as the platoon moved toward the village's center, the men were bombarded with rifle and automatic-weapons fire. The Japanese had just made it to the center of Morong, and Ramsey could see hundreds more Japanese soldiers wading through the Anvaya Cove tributary and entering the village. He knew that a charge was his troop's only hope. The shock of the mounted charge has for centuries been crucial to its success. The training of the 26th made it instinctual. Ramsey describes the charge:

> I brought my arm down and yelled to my men to charge. Bent nearly prone across the horses' necks, we flung ourselves at the Japanese advance, pistols firing full into their startled faces. A few returned fire, but most fled in confusion, some wading back into the river, others running madly for the swamps. To them we must have seemed a vision from another century, wild-eyed horses pounding headlong; cheering, and whooping men firing from the saddles.

The charge was a success, the last ever on horseback for a U.S. cavalry unit. But dozens of Japanese had hidden in the village and now had to be routed out. The platoon moved hut to hut, shooting through the walls as the Japanese across the river sent mortar shells over. One hit close to Ramsey, striking a horse, and he wrote of the scene, "It reared up on its hind legs with a horrible scream, and I watched its belly peel open, the steaming contents slithering out, and then the horse crumbled onto its haunches in a hypnotic slow motion."

The second and third platoons of the troop ar-rived and helped drive the Japanese back across the river. Troop E held the village until reinforcements arrived. Once Ramsey was relieved, he realized he had been hit in the leg. The horses were tethered in a grove by the river, but Troop E would have to move to the rear on foot. The sniper fire was so heavy that the horses, including Bryn Awryn, could not be recovered initially. However, the next day, despite the loss of one soldier, the horses were recovered.

Jaundice set in on Ramsey, and he was ordered to General Hospital No. 2 for treatment. Shortly after he left, the quartermaster confiscated the surviving 250 horses and had them butchered. There was no fodder for them, and the troops and civilians were starving. The horse meat would only last until March 15. Ramsey tried hard not to mourn the loss of the horse that had carried him through battle. It was a sad end for the animals, but to many it seemed an inevitable one. For Ramsey and others, it represented not just the end of their horses, but a move away from horse-mounted cavalry altogether. He wrote, "The cavalry was finished long ago. The army knew it; only we resisted in our pointless pride."

The battles continued down the Bataan Peninsula, many hoping all the while for the miracle of a convoy. It would be May before Wainwright was forced to surrender to the Japanese. The initial months of the battle were helped tremendously by the efforts of the 26th Cavalry Regiment. Wainwright himself wrote, "Here was true cavalry delaying action, fit to make a man's heart sing."

HEADQUARTERS
United States Forces in the Philippines

Fort Mills, P. I.,
7 May, 1942.

MEMORANDUM:

Pertaining to instructions contained in letter, this Headquarters, dated 7 May, 1942, subject: "Surrender.", addressed to Major General W. F. Sharp, Jr., in case of accident or serious illness to Colonel Jesse T. Traywick, Jr., G.S.C., Colonel H. C. Pilet, G.S.C., is empowered with the same authority.

J. M. WAINWRIGHT,
Lieutenant General, U. S. Army.

Correspondence from General Wainwright regarding the orders to surrender. *Gift of Jesse T. Traywick, 2005.169.*

HEADQUARTERS
United States Forces in the Philippines

Fort Mills, P. I.,
7 May, 1942.

Subject: Relief from Command.

To: Major General William F. Sharp.

            For failure to comply with written instructions issued you this
date, you are hereby relieved from command of the Visayan-Mindanao Force
and placed in arrest.

                                    J. M. WAINWRIGHT,
                                    Lieutenant General, U. S. Army.

Correspondence from General Wainwright regarding the orders to surrender. *Gift of Jesse T. Traywick, 2005.169.*

Mounted coast guard horse patrol. *Courtesy U.S. Coast Guard.*

5. Loyal Forces on the Home Front

The efforts of the animal forces overseas would be seen and felt with the many victories in battle and the ultimate surrender of Axis forces. The contributions of animals stationed on the home front were also essential to the victory at hand. Rationing, victory gardening, civil air patrols, and blackouts were some of the many things Americans at home were doing to help the war effort. Animals on the home front were hard at work as well. Though not in the direct line of enemy fire, many would have their lives put at risk for the jobs they were asked to perform.

PROTECTING AMERICA'S SHORES

After the bombing of Pearl Harbor in December 1941, Americans on the mainland were on high alert for an enemy attack. Many feared a Japanese invasion on the Pacific Coast or a German invasion from the Atlantic or Gulf of Mexico. These fears were not unfounded. The Japanese did launch over 9,000 balloon bombs, with a few hundred reaching North American shores. Japanese ships were spotted off the coast of California, and German U-boats interrupted shipping in the Atlantic and the Gulf of Mexico.

Military authorities felt it was only a matter of time before the Axis forces attempted landing operations. Even if the landings were not on a grand scale, small nuisance skirmishes could create widespread fear and panic. Therefore, the U.S. Army, Navy, Coast Guard, Federal Bureau of Investigation, Office of Civil Defense, and countless local authorities banded together to protect American soil from invasion.

Guarding America's coastline became the responsibility of the coast guard. The army was in charge of inland security, and the navy, of American waters; the coast guard fell in a natural place between the two. The modern U.S. Coast Guard began in 1915, and in 1942 the U.S. Lighthouse Service was also brought under the command of the coast guard. Its main function before World War II was to protect life and property in the event of trouble at sea. Coast guardsmen maintained navigational aids, such as buoys and lighthouses, and rescued survivors of shipwrecks and downed aircraft. Prior to World War II, in some sections of the United States the coast guard had already established a system of beach patrol. During the critical years of 1942 and 1943, the beach patrol system became one of the most

Seaman 2nd Class John Cullen, who helped foil one of two Nazi sabotage teams sent to the United States in 1942. *Courtesy U.S. Coast Guard Historian's Office.*

important elements of national defense, and extra patrols were created. In the First Naval District alone, located in the northeast United States, fifty-seven new lookout towers and outposts were created in 1942.

Beyond spotting ships in distress and offering life-saving rescues, the beach patrol formed America's first line of defense against saboteurs, enemy landings, and other types of espionage or "fifth column" attacks. To this end, the coast guard beach patrol assumed three additional duties during World War II. First, patrolmen were to detect and observe enemy vessels operating off the U.S. coast. From the very beginning of the war, German submarines were a menace on the high seas. Coast guardsmen were to report that information to the appropriate navy and army authori-

ties so that naval forces could be called in to subdue enemy vessels. Second, patrolmen were to report any landings of enemy ships or personnel. Finally, they were to prevent communication between people on shore and enemy vessels at sea.

The beach patrols looked for, and in many cases found, booby traps, mines, bombs, and other dangerous materials on the beach. They also aided in blackouts, making sure that homes, businesses, and cities were not visible from the sea. The beach patrol was to challenge anyone attempting to land. Patrolmen had the authority to fire their weapons over the heads of the intruding party, but they were only authorized to shoot to kill if those landing attempted to escape. The intention of these standards was to stop the party from landing; but if warnings went unheeded, then casualties would result.

German U-boats sank numerous ships, and fear of their landing saboteurs on American soil called for increased vigilance in spotting them off American coasts. Hitler did have a plan in place to create unease and panic on U.S. soil. He was eager to prove to the United States that despite their physical distance from the war in Europe, Americans were still vulnerable. Soon after the declaration of war, Hitler ordered his sabotage scheme to begin. Named Operation Pastorius, its ultimate goal was to land one or two teams of saboteurs in the United States every six weeks and create a network of spies and saboteurs on American soil.

The operation started with the launching of two submarines in May 1942 from Lorent, France. *U-202* and *U-584* each carried a four-man team that was to sneak onto American beaches. Each team was equipped with four waterproof wooden crates containing materials needed to carry out planned bombings and explosions. The men were also given some $50,000 in U.S. money for living expenses, travel, supplies, and bribes.

FBI mug shot of George John Dasch. *Courtesy Federal Bureau of Investigation.*

Items buried by German saboteurs, including time-delay devices, blasting caps, and detonators. *Courtesy Federal Bureau of Investigation.*

The team aboard *U-584* landed without incident just south of Jacksonville, Florida, on Ponte Vedra Beach. The saboteurs buried their crates of explosives as instructed and then walked along Route 1, where they caught a Greyhound bus to Jacksonville. The team aboard *U-202* landed June 12 on the beach of Amagansett, New York. The men rowed ashore in heavy fog and managed to change their clothes. They were halfway through burying their crates when team member George Dasch spotted coast guard patrolman Seaman 2nd Class John Cullen. Dasch climbed over a dune to approach Cullen and claimed that he and his friends were stranded fisherman. Cullen offered to take them to shelter at a coast guard station about half a mile away. Dasch declined. When Cullen became suspicious, Dasch offered him a bribe and threatened him. Cullen, armed only with a flashlight, took the bribe and walked away. As soon as he was enveloped in the fog, he ran back to his lookout station.

Cullen gathered others at the coast guard station, grabbed some weapons, and headed back to the beach. Dasch and his team were gone. They had managed to catch a train to New York City. However, by 10:30 that evening, their crates of explosives were located and brought to the coast guard commander and the FBI. A manhunt ensued, and eventually all eight of the saboteurs were captured. The first attempt of Operation Pastorius was an utter failure. But it was a close call for Americans; one team had landed undetected. The need to protect and patrol America's vast coastline was more important than ever.

Military authorities realized that the U.S. Coast Guard would need greater support and better preparation to keep more incidents like this one from happening. No animals were present, but the landings made clear that the speed of a horse and/or the keener senses of a dog would greatly enhance the coast guard patrol. Ongoing tension between the army, the navy, and the coast guard as to specific areas of responsibility had left the nation vulnerable to Operation Pastorius. From this time on, each branch would have to communicate better with the others and offer assistance as needed. As cited in *The U.S. Coast Guard in World War II*, a directive from coast guard headquarters stated, "These beach patrols are not intended as a military protection of our coastline, as this is the function of the Army. The beach patrols are more in the nature of outposts to report the activities along the coastline and are not to repel hostile armed units. The function

Members of the U.S. Coast Guard mounted beach patrol galloping along the Atlantic coast in an early morning drill. Though they worked mostly in pairs, patrolling the coasts for saboteurs, the coast guard cavalrymen were trained to work in large units as well as individually. *Courtesy U.S. Coast Guard Historian's Office.*

of the Army in this connection is not to guard against surreptitious acts, but rather to furnish the armed forces required to resist any attempt by armed enemy forces or parties to penetrate the coastline by force."

To increase shoreline protection and enhance communications with other military and civil authorities, the coast guard set up more stations all along America's coast and began regular patrols. Most patrols consisted of two men assigned to a two-mile stretch of beach. The men walked the beach together for their twelve-hour shift. These beach patrols were also tasked with keeping a vigilant eye on the ocean. Often, beach patrolmen were the only people in the area to give assistance when an incident such as a beach fire, plane crash, or ship wreck occurred. The coast guard beach patrols became eyes and ears for the U.S. Navy and the U.S. Army.

MOUNTED PATROLS

To perform the formidable task of patrolling the country's entire coastline, the coast guard utilized the greatest number of horses of any U.S. military branch during the war. Vehicles were scarce, and those being manufactured were needed overseas. So the coast guard requested horses, and in September 1942 the use of horses was authorized.

The coast guard's need for horses was immediate. There was little time to acquire, train, and allocate the animals. However, the decline in the army's use of horses resulted in a surplus of trained animals. Therefore, the U.S. Army Remount Branch supplied thousands of horses to the coast guard for use in beach patrols. The army's purchase of horses in 1942 was the last major purchase of horses by the Remount Branch.

The Remount Branch is the part of the Quartermaster Corps in charge of procuring and

Mounted coast guard horse patrol. *Courtesy U.S. Coast Guard Historian's Office.*

training animals and issuing them to units. The Remount Branch had been selecting horses for cavalry duty for decades. The selection process was therefore a standardized procedure. Soldiers looked at several factors when choosing horses and weighed the various personality traits of individual animals. The age of the animal and its overall health were considered first. In addition, all horses needed to have a gentle disposition, a good gait, and be of a sufficient size to carry the rider's weight. General parameters were about fifteen to fifteen and three-quarter hands high, and weight between 950 and 1,100 pounds. A healthy mouth was also key. Finally, the horse had to show courage and ambition without being too fidgety or nervous.

Horses were trained at various Remount depot facilities. At the onset of World War II, there were seven Remount branches across the United States

and three Remount depots. A fourth depot was added in 1943. These widespread facilities were a boon for the U.S. Coast Guard, since horses were available in all coast guard districts without the need to transport them over long distances.

Horses were ideal for beach patrol work. Their speed allowed coast guardsmen to run down enemies and make prompt reports. This ensured that more help would be forthcoming and that the proper authorities were quickly alerted to the presence of unauthorized persons. Often, since radio communications were not well established between stations, horses provided the fastest way to communicate.

The coast guard's Sixth District, which included Charleston, South Carolina, also encompassed remote, uninhabited barrier islands. Here, and along the open sandy stretches of the mid-Atlantic region, horse patrols were used almost

Mounted coast guard horse patrol on duty in the Sixth Naval District. *Courtesy U.S. Coast Guard Historian's Office.*

exclusively. They much more easily traversed difficult terrain and at a greater speed than a man on foot. Horses were also able to go places that a vehicle could not. It was only in terrain the horses could not safely cross that foot patrols were still used. In the Eighth District, the swampy bayou coast of southern Louisiana made both foot and mounted patrols impossible.

Night patrols operated in a continuous chain from Maine to Florida, from around the Florida Keys to Corpus Christi, Texas, and from southern California to Washington's Puget Sound. Where the danger of U-boats and landings was considered greatest, a full twenty-four-hour patrol was established; in all areas there was a twenty-four-hour lookout.

Early on, walking patrolmen were armed only with flashlights. But as the war progressed and instances of enemy landings occurred, they were armed with a rifle or a pistol. Mounted patrols were often equipped with both a rifle and a pistol, as well as with radio receiver-transmitter sets, a compass, and a whistle. One of their duties was to use the Coastal Information System to regularly check in with headquarters. They would plug into the established telephone lines along the beach, usually located about every half mile. Each patrol was given a certain amount of time to cover the distance between two transmitter hubs. Any failure to report in a timely manner brought an immediate investigation to that point.

In an emergency such as a ship wreck, horse patrols provided the quickest method to search for survivors coming ashore. The communications systems in place by horse patrols and the Coastal Information System were also the fastest way to report an incident and thus secure lifesaving assistance. The rescue of two people from the Greek ship *Louise* was directly related to the swiftness and alertness of the mounted coastguard beach patrols. The Greek steamer broke up in the Fifth District, near the Little Kinnakeet Coast Guard Station off the coast of North Carolina. A mounted patrol spotted the first of eleven bodies to wash ashore. Their quick response initiated search-and-rescue missions, saving two people from the shipwreck.

In the Eighth District near the Texas–Louisiana line, in the swamps of Grand Cheniere, army aviators were rescued when their B-26 bomber crashed. The plane crashed just off the coast, but the men became lost in the swamps as they looked for help. A mounted coast-guard crew conducted a difficult but thorough search of the swamps and found all the missing aviators.

The coast guard was constantly under pressure to release men from shore-patrol duties for duty at sea. In some instances, the U.S. government asked American civilians to step up and help with shore patrols. Those persons who had horses and

In 1942, the coast guard recognized that the use of dogs, with their keen sense of smell and their ability to be trained for guard duty, would help enhance beach patrols. Within a year, the animals and their handlers were on duty across the country. *Courtesy U.S. Coast Guard Historian's Office.*

Like horses, dogs were important to shore patrol. Trained dogs could run down and attack unauthorized persons on beaches. They even had a standard procedure to follow in case of an enemy landing. The capture of spies or saboteurs was essential to prevent the enemy from communicating sensitive information and from carrying out plans of destruction. Also key was the preservation of evidence, which would assist the FBI in discovering the enemy's intentions.

The beach patrol used about two thousand trained dogs in its operations. These dogs were acquired through Dogs for Defense and trained at the Elkins Park Training Station in Pennsylvania and on a 300-acre estate in Hilton Head, South Carolina. Like the army and marine corps, the coast guard accepted any breed for training. Dog handlers, patrolmen, and trainers had a few preferred breeds, including German shepherds, Doberman pinschers, and Airedales. The German shepherd proved to be the most adaptable to beach patrols.

Dog patrols worked primarily at night. In sensitive areas there was a twenty-four-hour sentry dog and handler on duty. Using dogs on night patrols took advantage of the canine's keen sense of smell and ability to detect movement. As more men were trained as dog handlers, dog patrols became increasingly common. Rather than a two-man patrol, a dog and its handler would walk together. This freed up personnel for more patrols and wider areas. The dog would work on a leash and alert its handler to the presence of something out of the ordinary. Dogs could also be a formidable adversary for any unauthorized persons. Leaders of the program believed that most people were more afraid of an attacking German shepherd than of a patrolman with a gun.

were experienced riders were asked to volunteer their time, horse, and tack to patrolling shorelines for the Temporary Reserve. In some parts of the country, once the patrols had been established, civilians continued to provide all that was required to make the shore patrol effective. For instance, in the Eighth District, which included New Orleans, ninety-six men and sixty horses volunteered for such patrols. The Temporary Reserve and its network of volunteer animals were vital to allowing coast guardsmen of this district to turn to other important duties.

The work of the beach patrols was not always easy. They often had to cut through thick vines and grasses to reach the shoreline, or cut paths through densely wooded forests. In some areas the beach was two or three hundred feet below a steep mountainside. Beach patrols took place regardless of the weather, so men and beasts were often exposed to the unrelenting sun and heat as well as the blustery cold, snow, and rain. Some coastal areas were rocky shores covered with debris, which could be slippery and difficult to traverse by foot, horse, or vehicle.

By June 1943, almost three thousand horses were in use by the U.S. Coast Guard for shore patrol duties. Almost all of these horses came from the U.S. Army. Although the army had relied heavily on horses for generations, jeeps, tanks, and other vehicles were making the horse obsolete on the newly mechanized battlefront. For horses in the U.S. military, the fight in the Philippines and beach patrols were their last major assignments.

BATS: THE ADAMS PLAN

The use of small incendiary bombs attached to bats to firebomb towns and villages was an idea proposed by Dr. Lytle S. Adams of Pennsylvania. Dr. Adams was a dentist by trade but dabbled in inventions as well as aviation. One of his most famous inventions was a rural mail pick-up system that made it unnecessary for a mail pick-up plane to land. This eliminated the need for landing fields and made pick-up more efficient. On December 7, 1941, Adams was vacationing in the southwestern part of the United States when he saw millions of bats emerging from the Carlsbad Caverns in New Mexico. Jack Couffer in his memoir *Bat Bomb* quotes Adams from a 1948 interview: "[I] had been tremendously impressed by the bat flight. . . . Couldn't those millions of bats be fitted with incendiary bombs and dropped from planes? What could be more devastating than such a firebomb attack?" Dr. Adams sent proposals for his project, and after some top-level scientific review, on January 12, 1942, President Roosevelt approved a plan to investigate the possible use of bat bombs.

The Adams Plan, as the proposal came to be known, called for millions of bats to be fitted with tiny incendiary bombs. The bats would then be dropped from a high altitude above Japanese industrial cities. Adams incorporated the bats' natural cold-weather hibernation pattern into his plan. Low temperatures at high altitudes would simulate winter hibernation, and as the bats fell they would gradually warm up and awaken. Once back at ground level, the bats would roost in places they felt most comfortable, such as eaves, attics, and other out-of-the-way spots. The tiny bombs would have a time-delay start, and would ignite as the bats were roosting. The small fires created would be hard to see, so they would be well established before anyone noticed them. This would make it more difficult for the fires to be put out, but would also give people a chance to flee unharmed. Adams thought such a plan would cripple the manufacturing capabilities of Japan without causing extreme loss of life.

Once approval came from the White House, the army's Chemical Warfare Service (CWS) gave the project a green light. Dr. Adams joined a team of field naturalists already familiar with bats. Conferring closely with Jack C. von Bloeker Jr. from the Department of Mammalogy at the University of California, Adams set to work figuring out just how to create the bat bomb. There were actually two main components that were developed separately. Adams, along with von Bloeker and other naturalists, worked on the bat side of the equation. Thomas R. Taylor, of the civilian National Defense Research Committee (NDRC), had been appointed by President Roosevelt to oversee the scientific aspects of the project. Taylor primarily worked on designing a shell capable of delivering a payload of bats. Dr. Louis Fieser, the inventor of napalm and also part of NDRC, focused on developing small incendiary bombs to be carried by the bats.

Bat expert Donald R. Griffin led the bat group in researching five main areas integral to implementation of the Adams Plan. Their first job was to locate and take stock of available species of bats. Second was to conduct experiments of the load capacity a bat could carry, as well as the ideal shape of the load and how best to attach it to the bat. Third, using a simple pressure chamber, they were to determine the maximum altitude and minimum temperature at which bats could survive and remain in adequate condition to complete their mission. Fourth was working out a method to transport and release large numbers of bats. Finally, the group was to investigate the necessity of killing the bat at the time of the incendiary's ignition to prevent it from taking flight and thus reducing the chances of starting a fire.

This proposed use of bats was the only wartime U.S. animal program in which the intentional death of the animal was part of the plan. Although dogs, mules, horses, and pigeons could die from combat injuries or illness, they were always of more value alive. The U.S. military did much to ensure the health of its working animals—except for its bats. In *Bat Bomb*, Jack Couffer touches on this subject. He was a bat lover from childhood and a protégé of von Bloeker, who made sure that when Couffer was inducted into the army he was assigned to the bat team. The Adams Plan called for one to two million bats to be used in firebomb attacks over Japan. Couffer states, "During such an extraordinary time it was natural that we would be indifferent to the ethical issues of killing bats as a method of waging war . . . if killing one or two million bats was an effective way to fight the enemy, using the method was not only prudent but was a moral obligation . . . and because of the perceived greater good I was ready for the sacrifice without a second thought."

Thomas Taylor at NDRC and Col. W. C. Kabrich of CWS began efforts to boost support for the program as well as to develop an incendiary device for it. By June 13, 1942, they had secured the backing of the U.S. Army Air Forces. In an official letter, Army Air Forces Commanding General Henry "Hap" Arnold stated, "The Army Air Forces will cooperate with the Chemical Warfare Service when experiments reach the stage requiring tests from airplanes." This expression of support enabled the bat and incendiary-bomb teams to continue pursuing their various goals in developing a bat bomb. However, it seems that many upper-level military leaders did not like the Adams Plan and doubted its practicality. Despite their reservations, work on the bat bomb continued, though both teams would be under immense pressure to produce positive results.

In researching the issues proposed by Griffin, the bat-team members ascertained that the bat most suitable for use was the free-tail bat. These bats were small but plentiful and easily obtained from caves in Texas and New Mexico. Their diminutive size was initially considered a problem, but the bat researchers determined that

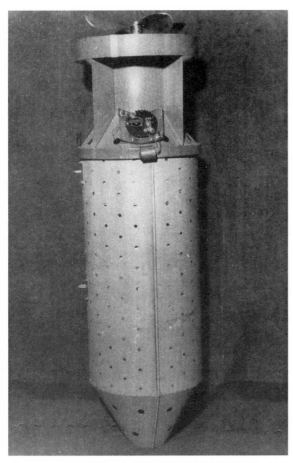

An early-model bat bombshell with mechanical opening device. *Time Life Pictures/Getty Images.*

chamber to simulate the bats leaving the plane. Although the bats fell from their perches, few suffered injuries.

More complicated, however, was the fourth of Griffin's topics for exploration—the transport and release of the bats. The team spent weeks bivouacked outside Bracken and Ney Caves in Texas studying the bats' natural habitat to ensure that a simulated hibernation could be achieved by artificial means. Eventually, the team custom-built a refrigeration truck to house the bats and produce colder, hibernation-inducing temperatures. This truck was used to transport bats once they had been caught.

How to drop the bats from an airplane also took considerable research, but eventually the team found a way to deploy them. They started with a normal-shaped bombshell and had it custom made to hold 1,040 bats. Inside the shell were containers measuring thirty inches in diameter that held each bat snugly in place, much like an egg in a carton. The trays were stacked one on top of the other, each bombshell holding twenty-six trays. The trays were connected at the edges by string three inches in length. An altimeter on the bombshell would open a parachute when it reached 1,000 feet. Once the chute deployed, sections of the shell would break away and the cartons inside would accordion out. The trays would slowly descend while connected to the parachute. As the trays separated, short wires appended to the three-inch strings would pull the time-delay device on the bombs attached to the bats, thus activating the time-delay igniters. The bats would use the tray at their feet as their launching platform. Safety pins on the incendiary bombs were attached to the bottom of the tray. Once a bat had oriented itself and flown from the bottom tray, the safety pins would stay behind. The bats' bombs were then live and on a time delay to ignite.

a free-tail bat could carry twice its weight easily, thus solving part of the second of Griffin's queries. The team developed a clip for attaching the incendiaries that mimicked the method by which a baby bat attaches to its mother. However, as the program progressed, team members learned that a simple adhesive was a more practical and efficient means of attaching the incendiaries. They also determined that a round bomb worked best. Pressure-chamber tests at the Santa Ana Army Air Base concluded that bats could withstand the pressure and diminished oxygen supply at 25,000 feet. Researchers allowed air to rush into the

A boon for the bat team was that almost every part needed for the bat bombshell was an "off-the-shelf" piece. A further help was that the bats were plentiful and easy to catch and transport. The major dilemma faced by team members was that the incendiaries not only had to be custom made, but some parts had yet to be invented. Dr. Fieser designed two bombs light enough to be carried by the free-tail bats. The bats themselves weighed ten to eleven grams (or about half an ounce) each, but they could carry fifteen to eighteen grams. Fieser designed one bomb weighing seventeen grams and one weighing twenty grams. The lighter incendiary was filled with napalm, had an exterior made of inflammable celluloid, and had a tiny time-delay igniter cemented along the side. White phosphorous was also considered as a possible incendiary material, but napalm was safer to handle and the quantity needed to start a sizable fire was small. The seventeen-gram bomb incendiary burned with a ten-inch flame for four minutes.

Once the bat and bomb teams had completed their research and tested their subjects separately, it was time to test them together. The first experiments were conducted at the army air force base in Muroc, California. Bats were gathered from Carlsbad and flown to Muroc. Couffer constantly readjusted ice in the bat cages to ensure the bats did not overheat in the May heat of the Mojave Desert. These tests did not go well for either team. The fire-starting capabilities of the incendiary were not yet dependable, and the bomber pilot assigned to the experiment would not allow the bombs on board in case the igniters malfunctioned. This eventually led to Fieser's development of the safety pins attached to the tray bottoms. Also, owing to the limited availability of metals, the bat team fabricated their initial design out of cardboard, which was too flimsy to hold up in the slipstream of the plane. Both teams went

back to work and agreed to meet a month later. Luckily for those working on the Adams Plan, no high-ranking military officials attended the Muroc tests.

The next tests took place about six weeks later in Carlsbad, New Mexico. Unlike Muroc, these tests were attended by an army air forces captain and a CWS colonel. U.S. Marine Corps General Louis DeHaven was also present, having been notified of the tests by U.S. Navy Admiral Ernest King. The location was favorable for the bat team, as it was close to a bat colony. It was also the site of the Carlsbad Air Force Base. Because of the top-secret nature of the Adams Plan, the team was allowed to use a newly constructed, but not yet occupied, auxiliary airfield on the base. The new airfield was complete with barracks, offices, hangars, a control tower, and several other buildings.

Dr. Fieser had not had time to make all of the needed adjustments since the Muroc tests. The new mechanical time-delay igniter was not ready; nor was the safety pin mechanism. The team was forced to use the chemical delay igniter and bombs with no safety mechanism. These bombs were fine for testing fire-starting capability, but they were not stable enough to load on the airplane. The team overcame this obstacle by advising the upper military leaders that sending armed bats over the airfield and the surrounding area was not a good idea, as the released bats could inadvertently roost and start fires in the local area.

The first trials at Carlsbad tested the effectiveness of the bombshell. The shell was dropped loaded with bats strapped with dummy bombs. The chute deployed as intended, and the bat trays came out of the shell accordion-style. Soon, the tiny bats began to launch off the trays in all directions. This aspect of the tests was a success. The team spent hours combing the area to find all the places the bats had flown. They found the bats roosting in eaves and barns miles from the drop zone—another success for the bat team. A second bombshell was loaded and deployed with similar results.

Unfortunately, the team suffered a serious setback during these tests. Fieser, who was producing a training film, wanted to put live bombs on the bats to demonstrate the incendiaries igniting. The idea was to cool down the bats to a semitorpid state, and to attach and activate the bombs with the chemical delay igniter before they awoke. Thus, the incendiaries would ignite while the bats were on the table. This way the film crew could photograph every aspect of the Adams Plan up close. However, the heat of the day warmed the bats more quickly than expected, and they remained in hibernation mode for only about ten minutes. Fieser had set the timers for fifteen minutes. As the armed bats awoke, they took flight. Before the bats could be caught, they followed the Adams Plan perfectly, roosting in the eaves of the airfield's buildings. Everything worked as it was supposed to—and the newly built, unoccupied airfield burned to the ground. Due to the top-secret nature of the Adams Plan, fire crews were not allowed in to salvage the buildings. It took only six bats to burn the Carlsbad auxiliary airfield to the ground.

Many army leaders were unhappy with the progress of the Adams Plan, and strife with NDRC eventually led the army to drop the program. However, the unannounced U.S. Marine Corps general present at the Carlsbad tests must have been impressed. The marine corps took over the Adams Plan in October 1943, and the bat team moved its operations to El Centro, California. In the meantime, Fieser succeeded in developing the time-delay igniter. The bat team continued researching the forced-hibernation aspect of the Adams Plan, now named Project X-Ray.

The last test for Project X-Ray was conducted in December 1943 at Dugway Proving Ground in Utah. Its objective was to make sure the incendiary bombs could start fires in Japanese dwellings. A few days after the marine corps' initial letter recommending a test, the request was also made that bats be used to "determine the action of the carrier, and the effect of the ignition of the incendiary unit upon the carrier." At Dugway, two replica villages were constructed, one German and one Japanese. These mock villages were built several miles apart out of the same materials, in the same manner, and in a similar layout to real villages in their respective countries. For this test, the bat team positioned the bats in the mock villages by hand. Hand placement was used since many thought the bat team had already proven its ability to effectively drop bats from the air and have them roost in the types of places desired. This test was a success, demonstrating that Project X-Ray was more effective than any standard incendiary bomb based on weight. Regular bombs give 167 to 400 fires per bomb load, whereas Project X-Ray gave 3,624 to 4,748 fires. According to the official NDRC report on the Dugway test, "It was concluded that X-Ray is an effective weapon."

Lt. Col. R. H. Rhoads had taken over as commanding officer of the Adams Plan when the marine corps was put in charge of the project. His report on the Dugway test dismissed the findings of Fieser, NDRC, and CWS. Rhoads wanted marine corps confirmation of Project X-Ray and its various tests before he moved further forward. Rhoads had by this point severed relations with Dr. Adams, so Adams was not present at the Dugway trial. In fact, Rhoads ensured that all ties to non–marine corps elements were severed. NDRC, including Fieser, and CWS had a tenuous status with the marine corps. Thus in February 1944, despite continued progress by Fieser and the bat unit, Project X-Ray was discontinued.

Several factors were cited for the project's

cancellation. Some believed that the fundamental idea of the plan was flawed and that reliable data could not be obtained. Also, many uncertainties remained regarding the bats' behavior. Furthermore, the team knew all along that the bats' natural rhythms ensured that they could only launch this type of attack seasonally. The bats spent the winter in Mexico and were not strong enough in the spring months to carry the seventeen-gram incendiary. Even with efforts to speed up the project's pace, it would not have been ready until mid-1945, a full year after it was terminated. Finally, the U.S. military had already spent close to two million dollars on the project. What many involved with the Adams Plan did not know was that another top-secret bomb was being developed at the same time, under the code name Manhattan Project.

SPIDERS

One of the most unusual contributions to the war effort by animals might be that of spiders. Spider silk was highly prized for its use in scientific and technical instruments. The scientific community had been using spider silk in their instruments since the 1800s, but as with other surges in manufacturing during World War II, the production of spider silk had to increase dramatically to keep up with demand. The military needed more and more silk for use in various instruments required for the war effort. Spider silk was used to create fine markings as well as sight lines and crosshairs on instruments such as telescopes, gunsights, periscopes, surveying instruments, and bombsights.

Several qualities make spider silk ideal for use in these types of instruments. First, it is durable. Although we often think of spider webs as flimsy and easily blown away, spider silk is actually one of the strongest materials found in nature. Dust

and other atmospheric factors make spider silk lose its tackiness, and thus its ability to capture prey in an open environment. But in a clean, enclosed environment, like that found inside an instrument, spider silk's durability is measured in years. Second, spider silk's fineness allows crosshairs to lie so close together that they appear to be in the same plane. This allows them to be focused together even at high powers of magnification, resulting in more accurate readings for the user of the instrument. Third, spider silk can withstand extremes of temperature better than other known materials. This quality is particularly beneficial for bombsights and other optical instruments for high-altitude aircraft. Finally, the wide variety of spiders and the silk they produce allows for the availability of almost any fineness of silk. A spider produces silk from two glands, of two different sizes. A good "silker" could obtain the size silk that was needed.

THE SILKERS

Tiny "defense plants" producing spider silk were located all across the United States. Some were in the "silking" business before the war, while others sprang up upon hearing of the need for spider silk. Most spider silk procured by the U.S. government for the war effort was from these operations, often consisting of only one person who cultivated spiders for their silk. One such producer was George Ketteringham, who lived in Cleveland, Ohio. Ketteringham was born in Lincolnshire, England, in 1877 and apprenticed as a young man to an optical-instruments maker in Ohio. While there, he learned how to manufacture and repair various optical instruments. During World War I he worked on the development and perfection of the periscope, and in the early years of World War II, he utilized spider silk for making crosshairs in various instruments. He

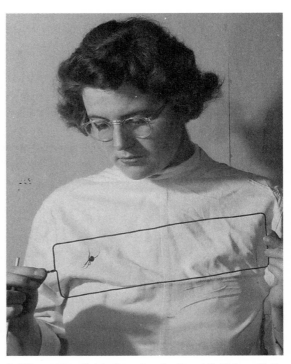

Extracting silk from a black widow spider. *Time Life Pictures/ Getty Images.*

Splitting spider silk into finer strands. *Time Life Pictures/Getty Images.*

studied spiders and their silk for years, and by the start of the war he knew which spiders produced the finest and strongest silk. In particular, he liked a type of garden spider that was "black with orange spots," most likely the deadly black widow spider. His neighbors would inform him when there were spiders in their yards, and Kettering-ham would use a handmade cage to collect them.

Nan Songer of Yucaipa, California, was one of the most well known persons extracting spi-der silk for the war effort. During the war years, several articles were written about her "spider ranch" and her need for black widow spiders. People from all over the country began to send her spiders through the mail, and the U.S. Bureau of Standards requested that she procure silk for them. She first learned of the government bu-reau's need for spider silk from an employee of

the American Museum of Natural History in New York. Nan had studied insects since her childhood, and once she learned of the need for silk she began collecting black widow spiders and their egg sacs. She fed the spiders and the babies that hatched on a diet of gnats and crickets, and soon the spiders began spinning silk. Nan's order from the U.S. Bureau of Standards required silk that was 1/10,000 of an inch. Once Nan had a silk strand, she split the silk into two or three strands in order to achieve silk that fine. She was able to split silk as fine as 1/500,000 of an inch. It took her almost two years to perfect her process. Although she liked the black widow spider for its silk, she also had success with the banded and golden garden spiders and the lynx spider. Nan sold her spider silk for twenty dollars per hun-dred feet.

In 1943, *Popular Aviation* featured a spider ranch in Fredericktown, Ohio, where two hundred golden garden spiders produced silk under the care of Emil Albright. Albright started silking spiders in 1937 when his brother, an associate professor of physics, needed help repairing school telescopes and other optical instruments. The operation grew, and eventually Albright's brother handled the orders and the bookkeeping while Emil worked with the spiders. He lived on a farm where spiders were plentiful. He stated that the spiders "thrive without any special attention from us."

Probably those least interested in spider collection for silking were the soldiers at Fort Knox, Kentucky. The army's Quartermaster Corps had the responsibility of procuring spider silk not only from outside venues, but from internal sources as well. The QMC sent soldiers out into the woods surrounding Fort Knox to collect black widows. These spiders were a terrible nuisance to troops training and conducting field exercises at the base. The soldiers were spared the task of actually silking the spiders, however. Instead, spiders caught at Fort Knox were transported to a depot in Columbus, Ohio, where each spider produced between 100 and 180 feet of usable silk per week.

THE SILKING PROCESS

Each spider rancher had his or her own preferred method of silking spiders, but all followed some basic rules. Healthy spiders produced the best silk, so proper care and feeding was essential. Spiders were well fed and kept in clean environments. Nevertheless, the silk-production schedules often shortened the lives of the spiders. For instance, the black widows sent to Columbus lived closer to four months than the usual year. However, while there, they produced more silk than they would have in their normal year-long lives.

Spiders were silked every few days. First, they were lured out of their cages onto various surfaces. Nan Songer developed a special pedestal system that allowed her to silk several spiders at once. Others allowed the spiders to crawl along the floor, spinning silk as they went. The silk produced was wrapped around a spindle. In some cases, this was just a wire coat hanger bent to facilitate the collection of silk, while other silkers made special spindles out of wire. Once on the spindle, spider silk could be further processed as needed. Songer and others who produced extremely fine silk began the cutting process on the spindle. Once the proper fineness had been achieved, the silk was cleaned of dust with a small brush dipped in acetone. The finished silk was again wound on spindles, each holding about one hundred feet of spider silk. Various instrument makers used the spindles to create crosshairs and focus lines.

The duties of animals on the home front were varied, but critical to the overall war effort. The protection of the coastline cannot be overstated, and the aid provided by horses and dogs was essential in the effort. Although many home-front duties did not place animals in direct combat situations, many bats certainly gave their lives in the name of the Adams Plan, and innumerable spiders had their life spans shortened with their silk production efforts.

A U.S. serviceman of the 27th Troop Carrier Squadron riding an elephant in India. *Gift of Dorothy Buzek, 2008.514.001.*

6. Foreign Encounters

Young men and women entering military service during World War II had little idea of the far-flung places they would travel. The typical serviceman and servicewoman had never left their home state before the war carried them to one or more foreign countries. Serving in the jungles of Southeast Asia, on the coasts of Pacific islands, in the deserts of North Africa, or in the waters of Alaska brought them in contact with novel animals of the land, sea, and air.

American soldiers in the China-Burma-India theater encountered many indigenous animals, including snakes, lizards, jackals, elephants, and monkeys. Some of the world's largest living land animals, elephants were used primarily as transportation and many times as subjects for photographs to send back home. Water buffalo were used nearly everywhere in Southeast Asia and on the larger Pacific islands for the tilling of crops, as transportation for goods and people, and, when necessary, as food.

In North Africa and its deserts, American troops frequently came across camels. A popular backdrop for photographs of soldiers with camels was the pyramids outside of Cairo, Egypt. This region of the world also offered Americans views of monkeys, small desert ponies, foreign birds, and big cats. When troops passed through the largest Pacific landmass, the continent of Australia, they likewise met many of its native animals, such as emus and kangaroos.

The Pacific islands could be dangerous with their plentiful insects and snakes. Troops traveling through the islands also had to be aware of the perils lurking in the shark-infested water. They often caught and displayed sharks as trophies. Other sea creatures, including octopi, squids, and sea turtles, were caught off the Pacific coastlines and proudly displayed as well.

On the opposite side of the world, troops were stationed in places such as Dutch Harbor, Alaska, where the average temperature is 38°F. Here they encountered large arctic fish and seals.

Despite its horrors, the war did afford many servicemen and servicewomen the opportunity to see the world and its variety of animals—perhaps a small diversion from their overwhelming sacrifices.

American Red Cross women participating in a ceremony with a decorated bull in India. *Gift of Linda M. Barran, 2006.150.*

U.S. servicemen of the 434th Bombardment Squadron riding camels with local Egyptian handlers, in front of the Giza pyramids and Sphinx in Egypt. *Gift of the 434th Bombardment Squadron Association, 2009.278.1359.*

Serviceman posing with a small jackal in present-day Pakistan. *Gift of Joseph Guy Thibodaux, 2008.513.001.*

Serviceman of the 27th Troop Carrier Squadron and his pet monkey in India. *Gift of Dorothy Buzek, 2008.514.001.*

In Faizabad, India, about fifty miles south of Nepal, monkeys ran wild along the train tracks begging for food and obviously quite comfortable with trains and their riders. *Gift of Joseph Guy Thibodaux, 2008.513.001.*

Members of the 45th Portable Surgical Hospital run into Burmese men riding adult elephants and leading a calf; notice the surgical unit's jeep in the foreground sharing the road. *Gift of Elise Feiner, 2009.157.261.*

U.S. serviceman posing with a camel as local North Africans go about their day around him. *Gift of the 434th Bombardment Squadron Association, 2009.278.1253.*

A member of the 4th Combat Cargo Squadron posing in front of Chinese soldiers using elephants as mounts.
Gift of Gerald Vessely, 2009.563.112.

Filipino youth ride a water buffalo through a small village. *Gift of Donald E. Mittelstaedt, 2008.354.327.*

Filipino residents butchering a water buffalo, or carabao, near Palo, Leyte, as an American serviceman looks on. *Gift of Paul and Barbara Canter, 2004.289.*

Members of the 2nd Ferrying Group pose while riding camels in front of the Great Pyramids of Egypt and the Sphinx. *Gift of Marion Root, 2008.366.001.*

Servicemen of the 434th Bombardment Squadron took this photograph of the working horses of the Sahara Bedouins they encountered at the El Assa Airfield on the Libyan and Tunisian border. *Gift of the 434th Bombardment Squadron Association, 2009.278.791.*

Member of the Ninth Air Force playing with a leopard cub in North Africa. *Gift of Marion Root, 2008.366.001.*

American servicemen posing with snakes killed in the Philippine Islands. *Gift of Paul and Barbara Canter, 2004.289.*

American military censors and members of the American Red Cross take time to visit native animals during their service in Australia. *Gift in memory of Col. Jerry T. Baulch, 2008.421.001.*

Members of the 50th Naval Construction Battalion (Seabees) stationed on Midway pose with their newly caught shark. *Gift of Sean M. Hickey, 2010.028.001.*

Naval servicemen holding a speared octopus on Ebeye Island, Kwajalein Atoll. *Gift in memory of Raymond J. Burns, 2010.124.084.*

Fish and sea lions photographed by a member of a quartermaster detachment stationed in Dutch Harbor, Aleutian Islands, Alaska. *Gift of Carolyn Reese, 2008.479.001.*

Sailors playing with a monkey near the naval air station on Bermuda. *Gift of Demitri Hioteles, 2010.013.001.*

The Pacific theater, consisting primarily of water and jungle islands, was full of insects unheard of by most Americans. The most dangerous—the poisonous or disease-carrying ones—could barely be seen. Others had the effect of intimidating soldiers by their abundance and sheer size. Thomas Roth, a member of the 749th Ordnance Battalion in the Philippines, described some of the native creatures in a letter home:

We killed a big banana spider the other day, it was in the toilet room and when Bob got up off of the seat his nose was only about too *[sic]* inches from it. It had legs 1½ inches long and a body as large as a quarter. There *[sic]* poison as hell and one bite is the quickest way to die there is. He let out a holler for some thing to kill it with and I left the garage on the double with the broom. That is the second one Ive saw since Ive been here. . . . I just saw a big snake crawl past the door outside, went out and killed it with (Bob's) shoe, broke its back the first crack and had to get a stick to finish him off. It curled up in a wring and couldn't get close enough with the shoe to finish it off then. There are lots of them around, they all look poisonous to me, so I don't mess with none of them.

Thomas Roth's letter home describing his spider encounter. *Gift in memory of the Betts family, 2009.295.018.*

Mascot of the escort carrier USS *Bismarck. Gift of Bill Christiansen, 2010.091.*

7. Pets and Mascots

The total number of animals used by the United States in World War II is unknown and perhaps incalculable when one considers the bats, spiders, water buffalo, and many other animals requisitioned along the way. All these animals, but especially the dogs, mules, pigeons, and horses, contributed significantly to the war effort. The stories relayed here convey only a small part of the service these animals gave. As a country, America asked the average citizen to step up and help: to buy bonds, to grow a victory garden, to ration food, and—the ultimate request—to send sons and daughters to war. But even more was given. Americans volunteered their dogs, horses, and pigeons as well as their time and expertise concerning the animals they loved and cared for.

These animals worked hard, often tirelessly, to please their military masters.

Animals' importance as companions, too, must not be overlooked. Although most animals served in a utilitarian capacity, they also provided friendship and comfort to the humans who labored alongside them. In addition, many units, ships, and individuals adopted pets or mascots in their travels. These animals provided some light-hearted relief from the drudgery and fear of life at sea or in a combat zone. Dogs and cats were popular mascots, but more unusual pets such as monkeys, donkeys, and birds were also adopted. In closing, we feature some of these loyal companions and friends.

Serviceman of the 434th Bombardment Squadron posing with a monkey on his shoulder, somewhere in North Africa. *Gift of the 434th Bombardment Squadron Association, 2009.278.1336.*

Naval serviceman posing with his pet monkey on Okinawa. *Gift of Rebecca Wilson Brunswig, 2009.608.024.*

Lady, a marine corps mascot, with the crew of the USS *New York* during a Crossing the Line ceremony. *Gift in memory of Grover C. Ore, 2009.059.036.*

Lady inspects sailors of the USS *New York. Gift in memory of Grover C. Ore, 2009.059.050.*

Catnapped!

CATNAPPED! That's what happened to Glamour Puss, feline mascot of the Camp Haan Wacs. Missing for nearly a week, the precious parcel mysteriously reappeared on the scene as a GI truck rumbled away. But the Wacs are asking no questions and paying no rewards. A steak dinner for the rescuer was the unclaimed prize.

'Glamor Puss' Victim of Mysterious Crime

Mascot of Wac Detachment Reappears but Reward of Steak Dinner Goes Begging

BY SGT BILL KENNEDY

Flash! Glamor Puss, the AAATC Wacs' mascot kitten, who has been strangely missing for more than a week—apparently the victim of a desperate "catnapping" gang—was safely back in his box today at the Wac Detachment.

The kitten's plight first was made public in the Daily Bulletin of June 17, when it was

Overseas EM Now Eligible for Bars

(ANS)—Enlisted men and warrant officers assigned to noncombat jobs overseas who have demonstrated outstanding leadership, but cannot be released for officer candidate schools because of the importance of their work, may now be given direct appointments as second lieutenants by their theatre commander, the War Department says.

announced that a reward of a steak dinner would be paid for his return.

The bulletin had been published only a few hours when a couple unidentified GI's drove up to the Detachment, tossed the cat into the dispensary door, and disappeared, according to T/Sgt Mildred Qualls.

Glamor Puss was none the worse for his experience, and today was frolicking gaily with his 65 girl friends, who were very happy to welcome him home. The kitten was a present to the girls from a member of the former ECP and originally was christened Glamor Girl—until certain discrepancies in nomenclature were discovered.

Anticlimax to the "catnapping" affair was the appearance of two other Haan soldiers who brought a large scraggly feline into the Wac office, hoping for the steak dinner award. They didn't get it.

Glamour Puss, a WAC kitten mascot, once catnapped, but later returned for a steak dinner. *Gift of Howard M. Curtis, 2008.422.063.*

Baby, mascot aboard the USS *Norton Sound. Gift of Artie Burnett, 2009.234.*

An older Baby, mascot of the USS *Norton Sound,* with crew members. *Gift of Artie Burnett , 2009.234.*

Monkey mascot of the U.S. Navy's Landing Craft Tank 1124. *Gift of David H. Steinle, 2002.459.012.*

Snafu, mascot of a U.S. Navy vessel participating in the Navy Day ceremony. *Gift of Eldon Lazarus, 2003.125.003.*

Ishma and Tina, mascots of the 434th Bombardment Squadron in North Africa. *Gift of the 434th Bombardment Squadron Association, 2009.278.737.*

Ishma in a foxhole in North Africa. *Gift of the 434th Bombardment Squadron Association, 2009.278.767.*

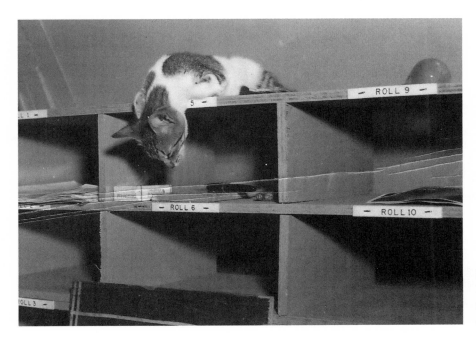

Honorable Kodiak Kat, the 73rd Bombardment Wing mascot. *Gift of Stephen Gerard, 2002.264.001.*

A U.S. Marine Corps mascot. *Gift in memory of Henry Glenn, 2009.233.244.*

Snopps, mascot of a headquarters company within the 29th Infantry Division. *Gift of Dennis Kirk, 2009.264.019.*

U.S. serviceman with his pet goat in India. *Gift of the 434th Bombardment Squadron Association, 2009.278.1020.*

Dog show aboard the attack transport USS *Bingham. Gift of Jane Killman Phillips, 2011.465.*

A small donkey helping to sell war bonds. *Gift of Regan Forrester, 2002.337.*

Colonel Sabodus, the mascot of an armored regiment in Italy. *Gift of Regan Forrester, 2002.337.*

1st Lt. Gordon Smith of the 870th Aviation Engineering Battalion in New Guinea with the unit mascot and one of her puppies. *Gift of R. L. Smith, 2003.167.*

Cockatoo mascot of an army medical unit in Rockhampton, Australia. *National Archives photo.*

George W. Schoeneck with his pet dog in France. *Gift of Betty Schoeneck Howell, 2009.630.020.*

Serviceman with a mascot of the 502nd Parachute Infantry Regiment, 101st Airborne Division. *Gift of Walter F. Zagol, 2000.016.004.*

SELECTED BIBLIOGRAPHY

UNPUBLISHED SOURCES

Oral History of Hiram Vance Boone, National World War II Museum, Inc., 2006.

Collection of Thomas Roth, in memory of the Betts family, National WWII Museum, Inc., 2009.295.

PUBLISHED SOURCES

"Army Pigeons: Hall of Fame." *Racing Pigeon Digest,* December 1998.

Bedini, Silvio A. "Along Came a Spider—Spinning Silk for Cross-Hairs." *American Surveyor,* May 2005.

"Black Widow Spiders Spin Thread for Gunsight Cross Hairs." *Life Magazine,* August 30, 1943.

Carter, William H., Gen. *The US Cavalry Horse.* Guilford, Conn.: Lyons Press. 2003.

Conn, Stetson, Rose C. Engelman, and Byron Fairchild. *Guarding the United States and Its Outposts.* Washington, DC: Center of Military History, 1989.

Couffer, Jack. *Bat Bomb: World War II's Other Secret Weapon.* Austin: University of Texas Press, 1992.

Daily, Edward L. "The Dawgonne Mules of Fort Ord." *Fort Ord Panorama,* September 1944. http://freepages.genealogy.rootsweb.ancestry.com/~gregkrenzelok/veterinary%20corp%20in%20ww1/dawggonmuleoffortord.html.

Downey, Fairfax. *Dogs for Defense: American Dogs in the Second World War, 1941–45.* Washington, DC: Dogs for Defense Inc., 1955.

Essin, Emmett M. *Shavetails and Bell Sharps: The History of the U.S. Army Mule.* Lincoln: University of Nebraska Press, 2000.

Glines, C.V. "The Bat Bombers." *Air Force Magazine,* October 1990.

Greelis, Jim. "Pigeons in Military History." World of Wings. http://www.pigeoncenter.org/militarypigeons.html. Accessed February 24, 2012.

The Homing Pigeon. U.S. War Department Technical Manual 11-410. September 1940.

Keeney, L. Douglas. *Buddies: Men, Dogs, and World War II.* Osceola, Wisc.: MBI Publishing Co., 2001.

Kemmerer, Bert. "Army Pigeon Still Rates." *Washington Post,* September 5, 1943.

Lemish, Michael. *War Dogs: A History of Loyalty and Heroism.* Dulles, Va.: Brassey's, 1996.

"Military Horses & Mules during WWII." Olive-Drab.com. http://olive-drab.com/od_army-horses-mules_ww2.php. Accessed February 24, 2012.

Miller, Everett Brunner. "Army Signal Pigeons," in *United States Army Veterinary Service in World War II*. Washington, DC: Department of the Army, Office of the Surgeon General. 1961.

Morton, Louis. *The Fall of the Philippines*. Washington, DC: Center of Military History, 1989.

Nicol, J. A. C., Lieut. "The Homing Ability of the Carrier Pigeon: Its Value in Warfare." *The Auk*, April 1945.

Pack Transportation. U.S. War Department Field Manual 25-7. August 1944.

"Pigeons Enlist in the Army." *New York Times*, February 18, 1943.

"Pigeon Fancier Finds His Niche in Signal Corps." *Chicago Daily Tribune*, August 10, 1941.

Putney, William, Capt. *Always Faithful*. New York: Free Press, 2001.

Ramsey, Edwin Price, Lieut., and Stephen J. Rivele. *Lieutenant Ramsey's War*. New York: Knightbridge Publishing Co., 1990.

Randolph, John. *Marsmen in Burma*. Houston, Tex.: Gulf Publishing Co., 1946.

Razes, Joe. "Pigeons of War." *America in WWII*, August 2007.

"Remount in Italy." *Quartermaster Review*, March–April 1946.

Risch, Erna. *The Quartermaster Corps: Organization, Supply, and Services, Vol. 1*. Washington, DC: Office of the Chief Military Historian, 1953.

Risch, Erna, and Giltsler L. Kieffer. *The United States Army in World War II . . . The Quarter-master Corps: Organization, Supply, and Services, Vol. 2*. Washington, DC: Office of the Chief Military Historian, 1955.

Rutherford, Ward. *Fall of the Philippines*. New York: Ballantine, 1971.

Sacquety, Troy J. "Over the Hills and Far Away: The MARS Task Force, the Ultimate Model for Long Range Penetration Warfare." *Veritas* 5, No. 4: pp. 1–18.

Southern California Coast Guard History Blog. http://cgbeachpatrol.blogspot.com/.

Terrett, Dulany. *The Signal Corps: The Emergency (to December 1941)*. Washington, DC: Department of the Army, Office of the Chief of Military History, 1956.

Thrapp, Don L., First Lieut. "The Mules of Mars." *Quartermaster Review*, May–June 1946. www.qmmuseum.lee.army.mil/WWII/mules_of_mars.htm. Accessed February 24, 2012.

Van de Water, Marjorie. "Crisis Communication." *Science News-Letter*, March 1942.

Wainwright, Jonathan M., Gen. *General Wainwright's Story*. New York: Bantam, 1986.

U.S. Army, Quartermaster Corps. *Dogs and National Defense*. Washington, DC: Department of the Army, Office of the Quartermaster General, 1958.

———. *Horses and Mules and National Defense*. Anna M. Waller, comp. Washington, DC: Department of the Army, Office of the Quartermaster General, 1958.

War Dogs. U.S. War Department Technical Manual 10-396. July 1943.

Willoughby, Malcolm Francis. *The U.S. Coast Guard in World War II*. Annapolis, MD: United States Naval Institute, 1957.